The re_____ mum v_____

SIMP_____ still ge_____

DISCOVER THE AMAZING PRO-OXY-GENATORS: New food supplements that help your body utilize oxygen more efficiently—to create more energy.

THE HIGH-ENERGY DIET: Now, turn more of your food into energy.

THE FOOD FIBER THAT INCREASES ENERGY by enabling your bloodstream to deliver more oxygen to every part of your body—including your brain.

PLUS: Ancient Yoga breathing techniques for instant energy. The latest stop-smoking discoveries. The end of the vicious cycle of tired body/depressed mood. The treatment of the Epstein-Barr virus—and other "fatigue diseases." And Secrets of the Energy Superstars!

DANIEL HAMNER, M.D., a specialist in rehabilitation and sports medicine, is a staff physician for the New York State Athletic Commission. On his weekly radio show, he discusses the latest health and energy discoveries (Sunday, WOR). He is editor of Peak Energy Press, a free newsletter on health and nutrition.

BARBARA BURR, formerly a creative supervisor and vice president in a major advertising agency, is co-author of The Runner's Repair Manual.

Read what the experts are saying...

HIGH-ENERGY PEOPLE PRAISE *PEAK ENERGY!*

PEAK ENERGY

**The High-Oxygen Program
for More Energy Now!**

Daniel Hamner, M.D.
and Barbara Burr

ST. MARTIN'S PAPERBACKS

We'd like to thank Anne M. Christopher, M.S., for her creativity in designing the menus and Enrique Loutsch, M.D., for his help at an important juncture.

"12 Questions to Help You Decide" from *Is AA For You?* Reprinted with permission of Alcoholics Anonymous World Services, Inc.

Published by arrangement with G. P. Putnam's Sons

PEAK ENERGY

Copyright © 1988 by Daniel Hamner, M.D., and Barbara Burr.

Library of Congress Catalog Card Number: 88-15674

ISBN: 0-312-92112-8

Printed in the United States of America

G. P. Putnam's hardcover edition/October 1988
St. Martin's Paperbacks edition/June 1990

10 9 8 7 6 5 4 3 2 1

Contents

1

It's What You Need to Get Everything Else

"I'm so tired from making a living, I don't have enough energy to make a life."

Too many people feel caught in that trap. And that's what this book is all about: getting enough energy to pursue your dreams, not just the bare necessities.

Some days, even doing enough just to earn a living feels like a tall order. At those times you especially don't want to hear about those annoying people who never seem to run out of fuel.

You know the feeling. You come home from a hard day's work—the kind that really takes it out of you, physically and emotionally. You have something to eat, and you remind yourself there are still a few hours left before bedtime. Maybe you could get to some of those projects you've planned: cleaning out a closet or using the rowing machine you paid over $200 for.

But you just don't have the spirit for it. Your body is tired, your brain feels numb. So you flip on the TV for a little relaxation.

On the business news, there's a feature about a 25-year-old who works a sixteen-hour day in his vastly successful electronics company, which he started when he was 19.

You turn that off and open a magazine. Here's a story about a grandmother who's running for Congress. She makes three speeches a day, confers with her campaign manager at 6:00 A.M. and catches up with her mail at midnight.

This sort of thing can be depressing. Obviously, these people were born with different genes.

So what should you do about it? You could simply say, "Well, some people have it and I don't."

Or you could truly examine the question: How *do* these people get so much energy? And is there anything I can do to build my own supply?

The question is worth pursuing. It's a fact that everything you want for yourself—a rewarding career, a beautiful home, more quality time with your children, travel, learning, even love—require abundant energy. Yes, I'm including love on my list. After all, it takes energy to get out and meet someone to love. It takes energy to keep yourself looking good. And it takes energy to maintain a relationship.

It even takes energy to have the happy, buoyant personality that attracts people. Your energy level has a powerful effect on your mood. You think better and have more interesting ideas when you're energetic. You're optimistic and more fun to be with.

Obviously, I'm not talking about compulsiveness, the driven kind of energy. I'm talking about healthy, happy, beautiful energy, the juice and spirit that help you rejoice in your accomplishments after you've achieved them—and *as* you're achieving them.

The feeling of being energized is such a fabulous one that some people destroy themselves trying to get it by popping amphetamines and snorting cocaine. But true energy comes from good health: physical, mental and spiritual health. I decided a long time ago that I would find out how average people can achieve that superenergy.

Today, in my practice, I deal with people who are intent on achieving their highest energy levels. My specialty falls into the field of sports medicine, but my patients are not professional athletes. For the most part, they're people who live their whole lives in an athletic way. They have high-powered careers and they also want to achieve in sports on an almost professional level.

New York, where I live, attracts energetic people; but right now the whole country is going through a health-and-energy explosion. We're witnessing incredible advances in medical science as well as a return to intuitive healing and ancient remedies. There are healers now who use hypnosis, herbal remedies, group therapy and revolutionary treatments created through cellular engineering—splitting cells apart and giving them new components, new patterns. The wisdom of many ages is coming together to give us health and energy never possible before.

The interesting thing is, the excitement we're going through now, in the last thirty years of this century, is very similar to what our country went through exactly one hundred years ago. If you were living in the 1880s, you'd be trying to keep up with vast changes that had been reshaping the country since the end of the Civil War. You'd be watching your world transformed by people who were both scientists and entrepreneurs. Bell connected the country by telephone. Edison expanded our days with the electric light and our imagination with the phonograph. For the first time, the entire country was linked by railroads. Before the Civil War, you might have lived in a small village where the metal industry was handled by the blacksmith. Now you saw the creation of U.S. Steel and Standard Oil—companies that combined the forces of virtually all the small competitors throughout the nation. (And we think *we're* living in an age of acquisitions!)

Just like today, there was an explosive interest in health and energy. An ad for a "parlor gymnasium" featured a muscular gentleman in long underwear—something like today's tights—swinging Indian clubs. These wooden clubs looked like long-necked vases. You held them by the neck and swung them around, doing various arm-building exercises. Not too different from Heavy-Hands!

Nutrition became big business with the invention of products like Sanka, Postum, and prepared breakfast cereals, which were sold on enthusiastic health claims. One manufacturer called his new cereal "Granola"—possibly imitating an earlier brand called "Granula."

Hypnosis was a popular healing method, and there was a burst of health-oriented religions. Christian Science flourished. The Seventh Day Adventists ran a sanitarium in Battle Creek, Michigan, which taught vegetarianism and avoidance of stimulants like caffeine. Today, the Seventh Day Adventists are once again leaders in advocating vegetarianism and abstention from tobacco, caffeine and alcohol. And their death rate from heart disease, cancer and hypertension are far below the national average.

Those thirty years between 1870 and 1900 boosted our country into a new world. The same thing is happening today. Once again tomorrow's world is being created by people with amazing vitality. In fact, just surviving in today's changing world—and enjoying it to the fullest—takes a lot of energy.

I may not have had this in mind years ago, when I started my energy search. But somehow, I've always been attracted to vigorous people and I've always tried to find out where they get their vitality.

My first "health teacher" was my grandmother. Until her eighties, Grandma ran a boarding house where she fed thirty people two meals a day. A lot of those meals consisted of fruits and vegetables she grew in a huge garden behind her house. She followed the teachings of Adelle Davis and Bernarr Macfadden. Grandpa, meanwhile, was off preaching salvation in tent revivals throughout the West. When he was home for a while, he built my parents' house himself, from 200-year-old logs, with the help of one carpenter. Grandpa was active till his death at 94.

My parents were very vigorous people, and I learned from them that energy was the answer to getting what you want in life. My mother taught Latin. She was an accomplished pianist and artist. My father earned his law degree through a correspondence course while working a full-time job as an insurance salesman. They both put a high value on education and sent my brother and me to a high school for overachievers. In my graduating class of forty there were eight or nine future M.D.s, ten lawyers and a couple of Ph.Ds. In that school you were an outcast if you weren't an athlete *and* a star student.

This was a private school—College High—the prep school for Western Kentucky University. Most of the kids came from wealthy families. I didn't. I saw energy and achievement as my way out of the "have-not" position.

I was probably a little compulsive about making something of myself; you don't know much about "moderation" when you're 16. My parents never had to tell me not to stay out late—I would never go to a party for three nights before a basketball game or track meet, and I never drank Coke or ate junk food. I played guard on the school basketball team. In track, I competed as a sprinter and jumper and became the state champion long jumper. I also threw myself into the Drama Club—probably a way of living in a fantasy world that was more glamorous than my own. I won a track scholarship to college, along with a scholastic scholarship.

But when I started to study health and disease in an organized way, in medical school, I began to feel there was no "answer" or "key" to high energy; I was suddenly overwhelmed by the enormous number of chemical processes that must take place before yesterday's lunch can turn into the power for tomorrow's track meet.

Later, during my first years of medical practice, my interest in my quest was renewed. I worked with patients who had extremely low energy, and I had the thrill of seeing depressed, discouraged men and women slowly build up to an average level of energy, and sometimes turn into truly dynamic people. At that time, I was working with Michael Schacter, M.D., a pioneer in using nutrition to cure tough cases of allergy, which can be very debilitating.

I saw similar transformations when, as Director of Rehabilitation and Sports Medicine at Dr. Robert Atkins' center, I helped sluggish, overweight people work their way into great condition.

Meanwhile, I wasn't exactly practicing what I preached. Especially after I moved into my present specialty—physical medicine and rehabilitation—I was "too busy" to bother with my health; I expected it to take care of itself. My diet was a haphazard combination of gourmet food and junk. I gained a little weight, so I worked out on light weights a few times a week, to fight back the flab. I had enough energy to do a day's work, and that was about all. Some days, I didn't have that much.

But for my patients, I was constantly exploring every new possibility for increasing energy. My practice puts me in touch with some of the most dynamic people in New York. Although people come to me with sports injuries, they expect me to do more than cure their shin splints. They're constantly asking for the latest medical magic to help them run faster races, play harder tennis, and still be stars on their daily playing fields: law, venture capital, entertainment and Wall Street.

So, for years, I've been gathering information from all fields, including Oriental medicine, yoga and herbology. I've even learned some energy secrets from four-footed athletes—racing greyhounds and racehorses.

At last I started to see that there *is* a unifying idea behind many energy-building techniques. Finally I was able to simplify and combine the knowledge I'd collected into a workable program. I tried it on patients, friends and colleagues. It worked.

And as I saw it work on other people, it became even more clear to me that I wasn't living up to my own program. I didn't look terrible or feel exhausted; but I began to wonder if I was missing something. Maybe I could have a great deal more vitality. It all came home to me in the fall of 1986, when I was watching the New York City Marathon. I had never run long distances in my life. In high school and college, the farthest I ran was 440 yards. But the energy of those thousands of runners was so moving, I vowed I would run a marathon the same time next year, and do it in under three hours.

The next morning, I went on my own program—as much as I could. I couldn't run because of a back injury caused by not listening to my doctor. So I worked out on a Schwinn Airdyne bike—that's a model that's designed to exercise both arms and legs. At first, ten minutes a day was all I could manage. That was November.

In January, I started running. I kept working more of the High-Oxygen Program into my schedule.

On November 1, 1987, I ran the New York City Marathon in three hours and eleven minutes. Three weeks later, on Thanksgiving weekend, I did another marathon, in Philadelphia, this time in two hours and fifty-eight minutes. I'd achieved my goal: I ran a marathon in less than three hours, one year after I started training ten minutes a day. And I'd run *two* marathons in three weeks!

On the High-Oxygen Program, I lost 16 pounds, which, in itself, gave me more power. My body now uses a lot more oxygen—that's the key to high energy. My oxygen usage was measured in September 1986—two months before starting the program—at 42.7 milliliters of oxygen per kilogram of body weight per minute. After following the High-Oxygen Program for about sixteen months, I took the test again in March 1988. Now I was using 56 milliliters per minute—an increase of over 30 percent. Of course, mine was not a controlled study; but the exercise physiologists who tested me were impressed at such an improvement, especially in a man of 48. We agreed that, in the literature on oxygen usage, it's rare to see an increase greater than 25 or 26 percent. And generally, they're talking about young people. One reason for my unusual results may be that most studies test only one way of improving oxygen consumption. I've developed a coordinated program that combines all the best-known, best-tested methods. This gives the body an ideal opportunity to reach its highest level of oxygen usage—and energy.

I'll explain more about how oxygen usage is measured in Chapter 5. The point is, I had seen my own oxygen intake increase. I had proof that my energy had built up tremendously. Now I knew for sure that my program worked, and I decided to get the message to as many people as possible.

You can read an outline of my seven-step program in Chapter 3.

My High-Oxygen Program is an important *physical* step you can take to increase your energy. But we all know that energy depends on your psychological state, too.

A child whose parents give him the message that he can do it—that he's a winner—has far more energy than a child whose parents teach him that you just can't get anywhere in this world; it's no use trying.

In your own life, you've seen many examples of how your mind affects your physical stamina. On the job, when you're involved in a project that's your own idea, and which you believe will succeed, you can work night and day. But when your boss gives you an unimportant piece of someone else's project to work on, you can hardly lift a pencil to get started.

Or maybe you're in your aerobics class, feeling too pooped to puff and huff; you've almost decided you should skip it for today. Suddenly, you notice an attractive woman (or man) in the class who's looking at you with a gleam of interest. Zing! You've got enough energy to kick and stretch for an hour!

Obviously, what's in your head affects the strength you feel in your body. The energy superstars—people with consistently high energy—somehow grew up with energetic attitudes.

Over the years I've absorbed a lot of these attitudes from the people I've met and worked with—and I've raised my own energy level by doing so. I wish I could put these principles into a simple formula for you. But our psychology is probably even more complex than our physical makeup. That's why I don't want to give you Ten Psychological Rules for high energy.

Your personality is unique. The best way for you to work on your mental attitude may not be the same way your brother should work on his. I want you to discover the psychological secrets the same way I learned them—by introducing you to some incredibly vital people—from the head of Apple Computer to a woman who's putting herself through law school at age 35. As you read their stories, you'll see what keeps them so alive and involved. You'll discover different ideas and techniques that may appeal to you. You'll find ways to use their approaches in your own life.

Yes, you can become more alive and vital; we know how to accomplish that. And every year, we'll keep learning more. Twenty years from now, "average" people will probably be doing things that we would find extraordinary.

Today, we're impressed by a woman like Carmen Jones, whom you'll meet later in the book. Carmen was bored with retirement, so she went back to work at age 61. All she wanted was a way of keeping busy and having fun. Today, eleven years later, the operation she started has become a multimillion-dollar franchise business. Thirty years ago, her story would have seemed almost miraculous. In another ten or twenty years, it may be commonplace for 72-year-olds to be creating new lives for themselves and jobs for others. Because this is the age of energy.

2

The Gift of Energy:
It's Free as Air

Instinctively, we all know that oxygen means energy.

Maybe you don't know precisely how your energy mechanism works—why you're sometimes wide awake and clear-thinking at 9:00 P.M. when you felt wiped out at 4:00 . . . or why you sometimes feel completely drained when you haven't been doing anything very strenuous.

Of course, there are many reasons. But, if you think about it, you've probably noticed that your energy level is often related to two things: sugar and oxygen. When you're tired and low spirited, you want sugar. So, even though you recognize the dangers lurking in butter pecan ice cream, you also know that sugar gives you an energy lift.

But there's more to it. Sugar alone doesn't boost your energy. It has to be burned in oxygen. That's the energy formula: sugar combined with oxygen.

Oxygen is another "energy food" you crave when you're low.

Think of times you've been in your favorite fresh-air spot—walking through the woods or along the shore. The air is clean and clear. You feel the urge to take a deep breath, to pull in as much air as possible. You lift your arms to take some weight off your lungs, giving them room to expand so they can take in even more. You inhale slowly and deeply, sending plenty of oxygen to your lungs and bloodstream and muscles.

Soon your body is humming, tingling; you feel light, alive and springy.

And as your lungs expand, your thinking expands: your brain is getting a rush of energy, too. Your thoughts stop running in their usual circle, chewing over the details of everyday life. You start noticing the sky, the earth, the birds and bugs—you feel closer to the source of life. If familiar problems do cross your mind, they now start to look like interesting challenges. And you feel very able to handle them. The world seems like a happier, more promising place.

What you've just been re-creating in your mind is the high-oxygen feeling.

Without question, your mind, body and personality are affected by your energy level. Whenever you get that healthy, invigorated feeling, you can't help thinking: this is the way I'm supposed to be. People with lots of energy feel like that more of the time. As a result, they act differently and their lives are different from low-energy people's.

Now think of a low-oxygen situation. You're sitting in a stuffy office. The windows are closed, very little air is circulating. You keep yawning, expanding your lungs to give them the oxygen they're asking for. Soon, you're so sleepy you don't feel like moving; you just sit. And because you don't move or breathe deeply, you don't take in much of the oxygen that *is* available.

In a very short time, you're feeling cranky. Your mind is befuddled; you can't think straight. Whatever you're working on seems difficult, annoying, too much trouble. You barely have the brain power to add a few figures or deal with someone on the phone. You feel less and less optimistic; your problems seem insoluble.

That's the low-oxygen feeling.

Anytime you increase or decrease your oxygen intake, you notice a dramatic difference.

When you give up smoking, you increase your oxygen supply and your energy goes up.

If you normally live in a low-altitude city, and you take a trip to the Rockies, you're tired for the first few days. Your body isn't used to working on so little oxygen.

The results of oxygen hunger were strikingly evident during the 1968 Olympic Games in Mexico City. One after the other, world-class distance runners turned in performances that were far below their usual standards. It happened in all the events that require big oxygen consumption. Working at an altitude like Mexico City's can reduce available oxygen by 15 percent for people who have not yet adapted to it. It's just as if they didn't have enough food.

You can't help wondering: If low-oxygen slows an athlete down, would a little booster shot of oxygen improve his performance? In fact, it does. Except where rules forbid it, athletes are often given a sniff of oxygen to revive them during a competition.

Oxygen tanks are kept on U.S. Navy ships that utilize SCUBA divers. And the other sailors on the ship—men who have nothing to do with diving—sometimes take a quick whiff to pick themselves up when they have to stand watch. The flood of energy is especially welcome when they've been engaged in debilitating shore-leave activities.

In affluent Japan, oxygen tanks are now available in some bars. People pay about $40 for a whiff of recovery. The Japanese who are truly prosperous and fad-happy even buy tanks of oxygen for home use.

Although it may feel good, we don't know the long-term effects of sniffing pure oxygen.

There's also a way of getting your body to take more oxygen from the air around you.

The air we breathe is about 20 percent oxygen. What we exhale contains about 15 percent oxygen. Obviously, we're wasting this precious fuel.

Professional trainers have found a way to get the body to *use* more; it's called "blood doping" or "blood packing." Here's how it works. Oxygen is carried through your system by your red blood cells. So what if you had more red blood cells; would you use more oxygen? Why not? Here's how I could give you more red blood cells: Six months or so before a race, I take some of your blood, separate out the red cells and freeze them. I wait a couple of months so you can rebuild your blood. Then I do it again. Twenty-four hours before the race, I give you back your own red blood cells.

When this has been done to professional athletes, they've used more oxygen, had more energy, and done better in the competition. Proof that it works: It's banned in athletic competition because it's deemed an unfair edge. American skier Kerry Lynch forfeited the silver medal he won in the 1987 World Championships because tests showed he had boosted the number of oxygen-carrying red cells in his blood.

On the High-Oxygen Program, you'll fine-tune your body so it uses more oxygen without blood packing. High oxygen doesn't work only for athletes. It's the key to vitality for all of us. The dynamo TV producer or banker or construction worker is running a lot more oxygen through his body every day than ordinary people do.

What about people who manage a heavy work load by taking drugs like amphetamines or cocaine?

You can read more about it in Chapter 18, but briefly, amphetamines disturb the chemistry of the brain and nervous system. They do not produce new energy in the body's normal way. For one thing, amphetamines increase your blood pressure by tightening up the blood vessels. By doing this, they probably decrease the amount of blood and oxygen circulated throughout your body. If you've ever taken an "upper," you know that the feeling isn't normal. You even look and act abnormal.

You may not know that one of your coworkers is on amphetamines or cocaine; but you will notice that he's tense and jumpy. He has extreme highs and lows, bursts of anger and irrational thinking. His state of mind is the opposite of the happy, optimistic attitude that goes with healthy energy. Drug stimulation burns people out. Oxygen-created energy keeps flowing in a smooth, steady supply.

So forget about charging up with one of these chemicals. Nature has filled the air with a natural "upper." And now we've learned how to use it more efficiently.

Oxygen is so directly related to strength that one way of measuring a person's energy is to measure the maximum amount of oxygen he or she can inhale and exhale. For instance, in one minute of breathing, an out-of-shape office worker uses about 30 milliliters of oxygen per kilogram of body weight. Compare this with the intake of a world-class marathoner: Alberto Salazar used 80 milliliters of oxygen per kilogram of body weight in one minute.

This means we can narrow down our quest from "How can I get more energy?" to "How can I get my body to use more oxygen?"

There is a way. Over the years I've developed a step-by-step program which anyone can use. This system can bring real improvement, even if your health isn't perfect, or even if you're exceptionally strong and vigorous to begin with.

Will it work for everyone? No. You should know that there are at least three obstacles in the way of natural energy production. You may have to work to eliminate one or more of them. They are:

1. Substances that kill energy
2. Fatigue diseases
3. Psychological factors

Energy-Killing Substances. Tobacco; drugs, including alcohol used to excess; refined sugar; too much caffeine—all these sap energy. If you can't eliminate them right away, you should learn to respect them and handle them with care.

Although I'm listing these substances as a separate problem— simply to stress their importance—they actually play a key part in the body's oxygen process. Most of them interfere with oxygen usage, as I'll explain later. Eliminating or cutting down on them is part of the program.

Fatigue Diseases. Underactive thyroid; difficulty in utilizing sugar; any number of food allergies—these are some of the conditions that affect energy. When you correct them, you'll see a dramatic change. Later, I'll discuss symptoms that indicate these conditions may be present. You'll need your doctor's help in correcting them.

But even if you do have problems like these, the High-Oxygen

Program can help you; it can give you an energy boost very quickly. In a week or two, you start feeling more energetic, more alive. And once you start feeling better, it's a lot easier to start working on some of your other anti-energy conditions.

Psychological Factors. We all know how much our feelings affect our energy. And, in my opinion, we've all spent too many hours focusing on what's wrong with our attitudes and self-image. So I'm not going to talk about what's wrong with your psyche. I prefer to help you learn from success.

To help you discover the attitudes that create high energy, I'm going to introduce you to some people who *have* the right psychology. They work and play long hours; they've made great changes in their careers. Some of them have created fortunes. They've all created joyous, productive lives.

Now let me tell you what happens on the High-Oxygen Program:

• You'll discover food supplements that actually increase your body's ability to process oxygen and create energy. These are safe, natural substances—not pep pills.

• You'll learn to eat in a way that "cleans up" your blood and gets it carrying more oxygen.

• You'll recharge your body with the most effective oxygenating exercises. Just fifteen minutes a day dilates and increases your blood vessels, so more oxygen-rich blood can flow through.

• You'll even learn an ancient instant-energy booster: a special breathing technique that quickly raises your oxygen level—and your vitality.

Some of these steps are effortless. Some take determination and imagination to stay with. But, if you do any part of the High-Oxygen Program, you'll feel benefits. Bit by bit, you feel more alive and vigorous. When you raise your energy 2 percent or 5 percent, you'll feel better. Keep going till you raise it 10 or 20 percent, and you'll feel fabulous.

Now, if you make the whole program part of your life and become a truly dynamic person, will you ever feel draggy? Will you ever have a low moment? You may. But that low spot in the day won't feel like a wipeout; you'll recognize it as a natural dip in the road, and it won't worry you. You know you'll revive soon. You'll become used to having an abundant supply of energy for everything you want to do. That's why high-energy people have the confidence to start new jobs, new projects, new relationships. They know they've got what it takes to handle them.

For too many of us, that feeling of confidence and vitality is rare. But it doesn't have to be. Human beings are not supposed to trudge through life; we're supposed to have the power to be fully present for whatever is happening; to be truly involved in our experiences, both good and bad.

And we're supposed to have enough juice in our circuits for laughing, playing and having fun. Life is not entirely about achieving things—it's about enjoying yourself, your talents, the people who are in your life now and the people you keep meeting along the way. That's the feeling you want more of.

And this joyous feeling is there for us, free as air.

3

Dr. Hamner's High-Oxygen Program

Getting your body to use more oxygen is the key to increasing your energy. There are many ways to do it—diet, exercise, breathing techniques; there are even some new food supplements that increase your body's oxygen-processing power. I've developed a program that uses all these methods; and years of research and testing have honed it down to the best- and fastest-working techniques. By following this simple program, you can increase your oxygen consumption in just two weeks. And you'll feel an unequivocal change in your energy level. In the next chapter is a two-week schedule for starting to work the program into your life.

The program has seven steps. Six of them fine-tune your body so it uses more oxygen. The seventh is about spirit.

Reaching your energy potential means reaching *your* potential. It means living your dreams now, not later. People with vast vitality don't stand with their noses pressed against the window. They've got the power it takes to get what they want now.

And you'll do more than just accomplish things. You'll expand your pleasure in life, every single day. Because having high energy simply feels good, no matter what you're doing.

There's a wonderful adventure, waiting just ahead for you. It starts with these seven steps:

Step 1. Discover the Pro-oxygenators. Pro-oxygenators are a fascinating new category of food supplements, as exciting for today's world as the discovery of vitamins were in their day. Here are the two I recommend:

- DMG (N, N-dimethylglycine)
- ginseng

Taking either one will increase your energy. Some people take both. There's a chapter on each of these pro-oxygenators to tell you more about how they work in the body, how much to take, and the success people have had with them.

Step 2. Exercise: Pump Oxygen, Not Iron. Not all exercises are equal in building your oxygen and energy supply. The real dynamo workouts actually increase the pathways in your body that carry oxygen. They get you glowing with energy in just minutes a day. Bonus: They even increase your brain power!

Step 3. Put More Power on Your Menu. You eat three, four or five times a day; but your diet may be interfering with your energy supply. Here are the foods and vitamins that clean up your bloodstream so it can carry a super supply of oxygen.

Step 4. Learn Instant-Energy Breathing. There's an ancient yoga energy technique you can use any time, any place. As you do it, you'll feel new vitality spreading through your body. This breathing method takes just a few minutes to learn and is described in Chapter 14.

Step 5. Get Rid of the Downers. Sugar, caffeine, alcohol used to excess, tobacco, amphetamines and other drugs can throw your power-producing mechanism out of kilter. Here are the easiest ways to free yourself from the downers.

Step 6. Check for Fatigue Diseases. If you're inordinately tired— not just an average person looking for extra energy—you should check yourself for symptoms of diseases such as low blood sugar, anemia, food allergies.

Step 7. Spiritual "Oxygen": The Secret Ingredient. There is such a thing as a powerful personality. Learn how to unlock your own vitality by watching five energy superstars in action. They all live the High-Oxygen Program; and each has a unique approach to life—an attitude that helps him or her surpass our usual definition of a successful, joyous life.

4

Getting Started:
Two Weeks to New Energy

The interesting thing about this program is that you can start with any of the steps you like and you'll still get results.

I think the best place to start is exercise; but you may prefer to start with instant-energy breathing or by taking a pro-oxygenator.

I have to warn you: You won't get full results until you take *every* step of the program—diet, exercise, pro-oxygenators, instant-energy breathing and developing the right mental attitude. If you exercise but continue to eat fatty foods, you're cheating yourself of energy. If you take pro-oxygenating food supplements but keep smoking, you'll never feel really alive and clearheaded. And of course, you'll have to get rid of other harmful substances like drugs, excess sugar and alcohol.

This sounds like a big order. But you only have to do it one step at a time. In working with patients, I've developed a two-week plan for getting started. Many people have found this outline an easy way to get into the program.

This two-week plan assumes that you have no exercise program now. If you're already exercising, and you need to increase the amount you do, you can make some small increases during these two weeks.

Before you start, make an appointment with your doctor. You don't want to exercise until you're sure what your heart is capable of. Your physician will probably want you to have an EKG test. If you're over 35, I recommend a stress test. It's also a good idea to get a baseline pulmonary test. It measures your lung capacity and how strongly you exhale air. You should have a blood test to check your blood lipids: total cholesterol, triglycerides, high-density lipids and low-density lipids. In Chapter 9, I'll talk more about high-density lipids and what level you should aim to achieve.

That first blood test should include a reading of iron and electrolyte levels in your blood. As you increase your exercise, you may have to take supplements of iron and other minerals.

As soon as you've made your appointment, put a note on your calendar to call your doctor again three months later for another blood profile. If you've been following the program, you should see a change in your blood chemistry. It really makes you feel good to know that you've made an important improvement in your body. The blood test will confirm what you'll already know—that you're feeling more dynamic and optimistic than you ever have in your life!

Now let's get started. It's fun!

Day 1. First, pick your exercising heart rate from the chart on page 90.

Then do one fifteen-minute workout. Be sure it's an oxygenating exercise; see Chapter 13.

You can go out for a brisk fifteen-minute walking/jogging session. Just be sure to monitor your pulse, so you don't overdo it. For an easy indoor workout, turn on MTV and do some dance steps, jumping jacks or running in place. At least twice during your session, stop to count your pulse for six seconds, as described in Chapter 13.

It's important to choose a form of exercise that's convenient. For instance, if the nearest swimming pool is so far away you have to spend an extra hour coming and going, you shouldn't choose swimming as your exercise. One reason so many exercisers have chosen jogging is that it's convenient; all you have to do is put on your shoes, step outside your door and start running. Other easy choices: a stationary bike in front of the TV set; an aerobics class that's close to your home or office.

Day 2. Read the vitamin checklist in Chapter 12. Review the vitamins you're taking now and make a list of what you need.

Day 3. During the work day: Identify a time of day when you usually go into a slump. Do some instant-energy breathing (see Chapter 14) when that slump occurs. Then get up and walk around briskly for a few minutes.

Outside working hours: Do a fifteen-minute workout. Check your pulse rate once or twice during the workout.

If you're a smoker, I suggest you don't try to kick the habit during these two weeks. Unless you're really smoking a lot—more than two packs a day—you can still get some benefits by starting the High-Oxygen Program. Work with it for a month or so. Cut out some of the cigarettes. When you start feeling more alive and positive, you'll be more motivated to get rid of the tobacco. At that point, exercising can be a great ally in your antismoking campaign.

Day 4. Go to the health food store and buy the vitamins you need. While you're there, buy some apple pectin tablets. Be sure you get tablets, not powder.

Day 5. Take a small jar of apple pectin tablets with you when you go to work so you can take some with any meals you eat out. If you usually eat lunch at your desk, you may want to keep a jar there. Take two 300 mg pills before a meal that contains fat or starch or sugar.

Isn't this great? You've improved your diet already—even before you've cut down on fat or sugar. Read how pectin does that, in Chapter 9.

Day 6. Do a fifteen-minute exercise workout. Check your heart rate once during the workout. By now, you're probably getting a feel of how hard you should exercise to keep your heart pumping at the proper rate. After a while, you won't have to keep checking.

If you haven't read the three chapters on pro-oxygenators, read them today (Chapters 5, 6 and 7). Decide which pro-oxygenator you want to use.

If you're abnormally tired, you may have a condition that needs correcting—low blood sugar, underactive thyroid, anemia. Read the chapters on fatigue diseases and see your doctor if you suspect you have one.

Day 7. Read the basic food rules in Chapter 8. Think about your breakfast, lunch and snack habits. Choose *one* bad habit you can change fairly easily. For instance, you might decide that, instead of having a cookie for your afternoon snack, you'd feel okay having an ounce or two of cheese. Or, at breakfast, instead of using whole milk on your cereal, you wouldn't mind trying skim milk.

Also: Go to the health food store and buy a pro-oxygenator. Start taking it.

If you have a weight problem, but you're not bulemic or anorectic, I suggest you start the High-Oxygen Program as outlined here. Make small changes in your eating. Start exercising, building your oxygen intake and getting more active throughout your life. In a few months, if you want to make losing weight an important project, you'll find it much easier because you're feeling better.

If you have an eating disorder like anorexia or bulemia, make that your first priority. See a doctor or get into a program designed to help you. When you're comfortable on that program, you can start working the High-Oxygen Program into your life.

Day 8. Change one diet habit at breakfast, lunch or snack time—just this once.

Day 9. Do a fifteen-minute exercise workout.

Also: Read a chapter on an energy superstar (Chapters 26 through 30).

If you have an alcohol or drug problem, get to work on that before you start the energy program. These substances are so powerful they obliterate the benefits of vitamins or exercise or good diet. Once you're on your antidrug program, the high-oxygen lifestyle will reinforce your progress and keep you happier in your new life.

Day 10. No assignment. Reward yourself; enjoy life. Make a date with a friend to go for a long walk and have a heart-to-heart talk. Spend forty-five minutes at a museum or gallery. Do some looking at new exercise clothes. When your body shapes up, you'll look fantastic in those shiny, silky shorts and tights! And your energy keeps building, you feel like walking, exploring and doing things, instead of flaking out!

Now that you've read the basic food rules, be creative about finding enjoyable ways to work them into your life. Substitute high-oxygen foods for fatty or sugary foods whenever you can do it easily.

Day 11. Do a fifteen-minute workout.

A word about exercise: People who aren't used to exercise sometimes tell me they feel *more* tired during their first few weeks of oxygenating workouts. When we talk some more about it, they realize that the "down" moments come only at certain times of day; at other times, they feel higher, more exhilarated. Don't worry, the exercise is building your stamina. If you feel tired, take a nap or get to bed earlier. In these early stages, you're building a platform. Once it's established—when you've got a habit of exercising three times a week and gradually increasing the amount, you'll feel your power steadily building.

Day 12. Read the ideas for good dinners in Chapter 11. Pick out a dinner that sounds good and that you can prepare without much trouble. Invite someone to dinner for day after tomorrow.

Day 13. Shop for tomorrow's dinner, if necessary. Buy candles and flowers.

Also do a fifteen-minute exercise workout.

Day 14. During the day: Buy a pocket calendar—the kind that shows a month at a time. Use this to plan your exercise sessions. At the beginning of the week, pencil in the days you plan to exercise. When you've done the workout, write it in in ink. At first, you'll just indicate that you've done your fifteen-minute workout. After a while, you may want to keep track of increasing mileages or the amount of time spent.

In the evening: Have your celebration dinner. Feel proud of yourself—you're on your way to a great new life!

Here's what you've accomplished in two weeks:

- You've started your three-times-a-week exercise habit.
- You've got a good feeling for how hard you should exercise.
- You've made a start on improving your eating at breakfast, lunch or snack time.
- You've had one healthy dinner—low in fat and protein, high in carbohydrates.

• You've read about the lifestyle of one high-energy person and you've started thinking about how you can use his or her attitudes in your own life.

• You've used breathing to give yourself an energy boost. Remind yourself to keep doing that—instead of eating a sweet when you feel low.

• You're now taking the vitamins necessary for optimum energy.

• You're using pectin to diminish the harmful effects of excess fat and sugar.

• You're boosting your oxygen usage with a pro-oxygenator.

I'd say that's two weeks of good living you've given yourself. Enjoy it and keep going!

5

Formulas That Light Your Fire: The New Oxygenating Food Supplements

A walk through a health food store is quite an adventure these days. On the shelves, you see products with names like Mega-Energy!, Bio-Blast! and Super Stamina!

Over on the book rack, you notice a pamphlet recommending enemas as the answer to all illness. Then there's a book condemning milk and a get-thin book in which the only diet consists of positive thinking. You can browse through books that claim to cure cancer through diet. Cure cancer with food? What a preposterous idea that seemed a while back. But today scientists in the medical establishment are conducting several studies to test the power of various fruits and vegetables in inhibiting the growth of cancer cells. They're interested in the effect of beta carotene, which is found is some vegetables.

There's the problem. It's hard to know which of the new ideas and products are well-meaning but misguided; which are out-and-out fakes; and which seem too good to be true, but *are* true.

Since my special interest is energy, I've spent years picking my way through the jungle of health claims—both in traditional and alternative medicine. I've tracked leads in professional journals and at conferences, especially those focused on sports medicine. I've read the literature put out by marketers of "energy" products; I've talked to researchers who are developing new formulas. When I find something that's safe and promising, I try it out on myself and on friends and patients.

Although, for my program, I've narrowed down my choices to a few formulas, there are many interesting and worthwhile products on the market—along with some duds. You may be interested in reading about some of the products I've looked at; they're discussed in the appendix.

For my program, I've chosen formulas that fit two criteria: valid testing has shown that they (1) increase energy and (2) increase oxygen usage. These formulas are called pro-oxygenators.

Pro-oxygenators are a whole new category of food supplements, as exciting as anything since the discovery of vitamins. That's because a substance that enhances your body's power to use oxygen can help your health in a vast number of ways.

How can we be sure that a formula is really a pro-oxygenator? Because it's possible to measure how much oxygen your body can use. Here are two of the most accepted methods:

1. We measure the air you're breathing, as it goes in and as it goes out. Air, as you know, is composed of about 20 percent oxygen and 80 percent other gases—mostly nitrogen.

Now, if I analyze the air before you inhale and find that 18 percent of it is oxygen; then analyze it again as you exhale, and it's 15 percent oxygen—I know how much oxygen you've used. Naturally, if you have a bigger body, you use more oxygen. And if you're exercising hard, you use more oxygen than if you're sitting still. The harder you work, the more oxygen you use. So the test for maximum oxygen usage is done while you're running on a treadmill. You have pincers on your nose and you breathe into a mask. You run till you're exhausted—that way, we know you've used the largest volume of oxygen you're capable of using.

We calculate your oxygen-usage rate in terms of the amount of oxygen you used in a certain time, and it's related to how much you weigh. The rate is called your $VO_2 MAX$. (V for volume, O_2 for oxygen, MAX for maximum.) For instance, your $VO_2 MAX$ might be 40. That means you use 40 milliliters of oxygen per kilogram of body weight in one minute—when you're exercising at your maximum.

2. Another method: We measure the amount of lactic acid in your blood after exercise. This is an indirect method that gives an

indication of whether you've used more or less oxygen. What does lactic acid have to do with oxygen usage? Lactic acid is a waste product the body throws off when you're running low on oxygen. When your muscles are so tired they hurt, you're feeling the results of lactic acid.

Suppose you're biking or swimming and your body can't process enough oxygen to create the energy the activity demands; your body then finds a way of making energy with less oxygen. This is an inefficient way and in the process the body produces lactic acid. Actually, that's good, in a way. The lactic acid interferes with muscle contraction and makes your muscles hurt. Eventually, the muscle cramps; it won't relax after a contraction. Then you have to stop exercising.

If we find a high percentage of lactic acid in your blood after exercise, we know you've run low on oxygen. Suppose we tested you again a week later and found you'd produced less lactic acid after the same amount of exercise. Then we'd know you'd been using *more* oxygen to create energy.

Because we can measure your oxygen usage, we can test ways of getting you to use more. One of these ways is to take a food supplement that's a pro-oxygenator.

Of all the supplements I've examined, the two I like best are DMG and ginseng. I'll tell you all about them in the next two chapters. I've tried them myself and on a number of patients, colleagues and friends. Before I ever tried them, they'd been tested and studied for years. They've demonstrated their ability to increase endurance, lessen recovery time and make you react faster. They can even help your mental alertness and mood.

I know many people who take one or the other, and some who take both. I take both. That's because my guess is, they work differently and give somewhat different benefits. Although both have been tested extensively and continue to be studied, we don't know everything about how they work. For instance, ginseng has shown its ability to improve certain mental functions. Koreans and other Asians use ginseng for stamina and overall health. In the martial arts world, Koreans are known to have incredible endurance. Some people give the credit to Korean ginseng; others say it's because they eat so much garlic!

DMG (N, N-dimethylglycine) is used by both human and four-footed athletes to keep them running at their top speed for longer periods of time. Some cardiologists have found it helps normalize heart rhythm. It even has patents for its power to strengthen the immune system.

So, until we know more about these two formulas, I'm betting they have somewhat different properties. They're both safe to use. Read about them and try the one that appeals to you. You may want to try one for a few months, and then the other.

One of the fascinating facts about these pro-oxygenators is that they've shown such a wide variety of benefits. Ginseng, for instance, has been credited for centuries with an ability to enhance performance in arenas ranging from the battlefield to the bedroom.

When you hear that, you may start to feel skeptical. Maybe it's all a myth. How can one substance work in so many ways? But think again and you'll realize it isn't so far-fetched. For instance, if you had a product that strengthened your immune system, think what it could do. It would help you fight off colds and flu; it might keep you from being allergic to industrial pollutants, like air-borne petroleum, keep you from having reactions to irritating cosmetics or perfume and from sneezing during hay fever season. These problems seem unrelated until you understand the idea of the immune system.

Or suppose there's something like a "master gland." The pituitary is often called the master gland. The pituitary is located in the brain; it's part of the endocrine system. It produces and releases several hormones that influence such things as the heartbeat, overall body temperature and various stress reactions. So anything that strengthens or weakens the pituitary gland causes ripple effects throughout the body.

I'm not saying that ginseng or DMG affect the pituitary gland; we don't know exactly what core function they work on. But they do affect many processes, and some researchers believe they're adaptogens.

Adaptogens are a fairly new idea that scientists are discussing. We're beginning to look at substances that work on basic body functions that affect many other reactions. An adaptogen would work to keep all systems normal—not too high or too low. It wouldn't "over correct" or cause side reactions as many drugs do. It would help keep the body on an even keel in the face of many challenges, such as viruses, fatigue, extreme heat or cold, or noise; it would help you survive toxic substances such as alcohol and other drugs; it would even help keep you from overreacting, physically, to emotional stresses.

This search for a generalized action that keeps the body normal is very different from Western medicine's traditional approach. We're used to treating isolated problems. Eastern medicine has always seen overall health as the goal. Herbal remedies, acupuncture, yoga postures—even meditation—all aim for balance, homeostasis. Maybe that's why the idea of adaptogens has been accepted in China, Japan and Russia more easily than in the West.

Germanium, a substance that seems to be an adaptogen, is one of the most popular medicines in Japan. Siberian Ginseng is widely accepted in the Soviet Union; Russian studies report its power to help people withstand a great variety of stresses. In fact, the ginseng plant has been known for centuries as an overall strengthener and a cure for a variety of problems.

Another apparent adaptogen you'll read about in this book— DMG—does such diverse things as reducing the frequency of epileptic seizures, increasing resistance to pneumonia and lowering cholesterol.

It's my belief that DMG and ginseng are adaptogens.

Whether they are or not, it's been well demonstrated that they're pro-oxygenators—they help your body use more oxygen. Oxygen affects so many functions in the body, that alone would account for their ability to help you in many ways.

But What About Antioxidants?

While we're on the subject of oxygen: You may have read about *anti*oxidants—chemicals that are believed to fight aging and stress.

Antioxidants help you by taking care of unbalanced molecules—molecules that have an extra atom of oxygen with a negative charge. These "unblanced molecules" are called free radicals.

Molecules are always seeking to stay in balance, with an equal number of positive and negative atoms. But some normal functions of the body—such as the breakdown of fats—produce oxygen atoms with a negative charge. This negative atom looks around for a molecule with a positive atom that it can hook onto. As soon as it does so, the molecule is unbalanced. It has to find another molecule to connect to. This "hooking up" or linking together of unbalanced molecules causes damage in the body. The remedy seems to be: find something to link onto that negative oxygen atom and neutralize it. That "something" is called an antioxidant.

So when I tell you to increase the oxygen your body uses, I'm not telling you to increase an oxygen atom with a negative charge. I'm telling you to increase your usage of O_2, a balanced, stable molecule of oxygen. This is the normal, healthy oxygen you breathe in the air. It's part of our natural fuel system. O_2 is what helps you feel alive and positive and ready to win the world. Pro-oxygenators are one way of getting your body to use more of it.

6

DMG: It turns Faders into Finishers

I learned a new word when I first started reading about the food supplement called DMG. The word is "fader."

A racing greyhound that's capable of high speeds but can't maintain his top speed for long is known as a fader. He starts strong, but fades before the race is finished.

When DMG was given to racing greyhounds, the trainers noted that the dogs didn't increase their maximum speed; but they *maintained* their maximum speeds for a longer period. Instead of fading, they kept giving the best they were capable of, right to the end of the race.

When I read these test results, I had to put down the journal for a moment. I kept thinking: what a wonderful contribution this could be to human lives!

Most of us know what it's like to perform at our best—you enjoy your work, you keep coming up with new ideas; you feel so good you can even be more patient with difficult people.

But somehow, those peak times don't last. You slow down or get discouraged by a setback and you go into a slump. You fade. Some days, you have barely enough energy to put in an adequate performance; you're just getting the job done.

If only you could stay at your peak—think how much more enjoyable your life would be. And how much healthier your career would be!

Well, it turns out, DMG *does* help humans stay at their peak longer. It sustains our energy—as well as greyhounds'—by increasing the amount of oxygen we use.

What is DMG?

DMG is a natural substance found in meat, seeds and grains. We also produce it in our own bodies, but it soon becomes something else. The body is constantly forming chemicals it needs as a step toward forming other chemicals—they're intermediate steps in creating what the body needs. These short-lived chemicals are called intermediate metabolites. DMG is one of these.

Since DMG plays a temporary role in a cycle, we don't store it and we don't know of any deficiency symptoms directly related to lack of it. This doesn't mean it's not essential to keeping the body running efficiently. DMG occupies a central position in a metabolic pathway that has impact on all other major cycles in the body, such as the metabolism of proteins and fats and carbohydrates. So you can think of DMG as a worker at a key point in the assembly line. If you weaken or strengthen that worker, you can affect all sorts of things further down the line. One of the things affected is our power to use oxygen.

DMG's oxygen-boosting power has far-reaching health benefits, besides its effect on energy. Oxygen is involved in the functioning of every cell in the body. And DMG's action has brought dramatic improvement to patients whose low oxygen usage is actually life threatening.

Heart patients, for instance, can't pump enough oxygen-carrying blood to supply the basic needs of the body.

People with poor circulation suffer a variety of problems—from coldness and numbness in the extremities to having their feet turn blue from a shortage of oxygen-rich blood.

Diabetics need oxygen to digest sugar more efficiently.

DMG's success in treating these conditions has been reported in studies done here and in the Soviet Union. And the same oxygen enhancement that helps people with heart trouble or poor circulation can help anyone who wants more energy.

Can it help you perform better on the job? I'm sure it can. But,

41

as you can imagine, it's hard to measure exactly how energetically you're working in the office or classroom. The easiest thing to test is pure physical vigor. In this area DMG has proven itself with flying colors. In fact, its test results are so exciting it's now used by teams and individual athletes—people whose livelihood depends on having a bit more staying power than the next guy.

The list includes the Dallas Cowboys and the New England Patriots; the Dolphins' Robert Kutchenburg and the L.A. Rams' Jack Youngblood, now retired. It's used by coaches and trainers like Gary Giemont of the L.A. Rams and Dick Brown of the Athletics West running club.

Runners like Joan Benoit Samuelson, Mary Decker Slaney and Alberto Salazar use DMG; and so does a runner you'll meet later in this book, Henry Marsh. Henry is both an Olympic athlete and an attorney—two occupations that require exceptionally high stamina and spirit.

Stacy Creamer, one of the editors at Putnam, is an avid runner. She read an early draft of *Peak Energy* and decided to try DMG. Six weeks after including it in her diet, she achieved a new personal best, running a 10-kilometer race (6.2 miles) in less than forty minutes. This goal had been just beyond her grasp for more than nine months. Since she always lives the High-Oxygen Program, in terms of diet, exercise and other factors, she credits DMG with her new level of energy.

DMG is even used by four-footed athletes. Racehorses take it in a product called Vetricine, which is used by trainers throughout the country. In fact, some of DMG's most interesting performance tests have been done on animal runners—such as the racing greyhounds I mentioned earlier. These greyhounds are ideal test subjects because they're so carefully bred and controlled for weight and size. They're about the most standardized characters you can find. Racehorses have much greater size variations, as do humans. So greyhounds are perfect subjects for testing a substance like DMG.

Another thing I like about testing substances on animals, as opposed to humans, is that there's no chance of a "placebo effect." The placebo effect is what happens when you give someone a dummy pill—a placebo—and they recover from their illness or feel stronger simply because they *believe* they've taken something that will help. I'm convinced that greyhounds and laboratory rats don't know they've been given a food supplement in their food or drinking water; so when they have more energy, it must be the supplement that's working. And that's what's happened in the case of DMG. Here are some results of tests with both humans and animals:

• College athletes increased their oxygen usage (VO_2 MAX) when using DMG. Half the subjects were given DMG; half were given a placebo. After two weeks, the pills were switched. In each case, the men's VO_2 MAX increased when they used DMG and went back to its previous level when they were taking the placebo.

The men who took part in this test were young and in great shape. It's easy enough to get some improvement in a subject who's a blob to begin with; but if you can get a top athlete to perform even *better*—then you've got an effective product.

• Laboratory rats who were fed DMG ran longer before they stopped from exhaustion than rats who didn't get DMG. To make the test even tougher, the rats were put in an oxygen-poor environment. The air in their glass rooms was altered to make it low in oxygen. Even under these conditions, the DMG-fed rats surpassed the others. This test was done at the University of Southern California by Jerzy Meduski, M.D.

• Racing greyhounds' times were recorded in trials on metropolitan race tracks over a three-week period. Then for the next five days, they were given DMG. Every single greyhound showed improved performance in terms of stamina; they stayed at their top speeds longer. The faders became finishers!

• When members of a track team were given DMG, they showed an average increase of 27 percent in VO_2 MAX and they could run 23.6 percent longer before they felt so tired they had to stop.

• Racing thoroughbreds showed less lactic acid in their blood after exercise than horses that did not take DMG. Rabbits placed under stress produced less lactic acid.

Although I first got interested in DMG because of its energy-enhancement powers, I kept discovering fascinatingly diverse attributes.

A cardiologist tried DMG on three hundred patients. He found improvement in people with an irregular heartbeat. Patients with coronary insufficiency got better. High-cholesterol and high-triglyceride counts were lowered. And many patients said they simply felt better—more vigorous and optimistic. The doctor himself started taking DMG and says he feels more energetic.

Other interesting results reported for DMG include its ability to decrease the frequency of epileptic seizures and strengthen the immune system. In fact, it has two patents for its ability to strengthen the immune response.

Immune-system strengthening can be important to you if you're just starting an exercise program. New exercisers get enthusiastic and push themselves too hard; then they break down. They become susceptible to colds and sore throats and any bug that's around. Even experienced athletes have trouble finding the line between good vigorous exertion and "overdoing it"; Olympic athletes often have enforced vacations, due to colds, when they're trying for new limits. Since DMG has immunity-enhancing powers, it could help protect you from "overtraining illnesses"—besides increasing your energy.

It's this wide variety of properties that makes me feel that DMG may well be an adaptogen.

The product used in these tests is sold as Aangamik DMG. It's marketed by FoodScience Laboratories. You'll find it in most health food stores. There are other brands of DMG, and they may be identical in their purity and power. If you see another brand you're curious about, write the company and ask what studies they've done. Manufacturers are always happy to tell you good things about their product.

How Much Should You Take?

The Aangamik manufacturer suggests 250 mg per day—that's one tablet with breakfast, one about 5:00 P.M. If you're doing a lot of exercise or you're under extra stress, you can use more. In some cases, athletes have used 800 mg daily.

You can expect results in a few weeks. Some people feel the difference in days. Whether you're a salesman or a runner or you get your mileage by chasing kids all day, DMG can give you a boost of what you need—more oxygen and energy.

7

Ginseng: An Oriental Mystery Story

Ginseng has the power to prolong life, cure illnesses ranging from indigestion to memory lapse, and rev up your sexual powers.

True or false?

Ginseng is the original energy booster and has a four-thousand-year track record for bestowing extraordinary strength on warriors and workers alike.

Fact? Or superstition?

For centuries, near-magical properties have been ascribed to ginseng. It was given to soldiers to build their endurance in battle. Some of the oldest medical texts, such as a Chinese treatise written in A.D. 200, prescribe it for a wide variety of ailments. In 1697, the Paris Academy of Sciences discussed its aphrodisiac powers, and the rumors must have spread; a few years later, the French court was criticized for being caught up in a scandalous "ginseng madness."

As its popularity spread, the plant was cultivated in many countries, including the United States. The Canadian Indians used it as a medicine. The Dutch used it for restoring strength after illness. Today, with the great increase in America's Oriental population, ginseng is even more widely available than ever. In Kentucky, where I grew up, ginseng is a popular commercial crop.

Yet many people have tried ginseng as an energy booster and have been disappointed; either it made them nervous and hyperactive or it seemed to give no results at all. Researchers who tested ginseng have also reported mixed results.

In spite of its uneven reputation, I've always been curious about this little plant. After all, ancient Oriental medicine has given us other valuable therapies that were not accepted at first. Chinese medicine used mold as a cure long before we discovered its active ingredient, penicillin. Acupuncture was scorned by Westerners for years; now many M.D.s take courses in it.

And modern Asians continue to use ginseng as a matter of course, to build strength and stamina. During the Soviet occupation of Korea in 1945, the Russians observed the North Koreans' use of ginseng and took some plants to the Soviet Union for testing. They must have been impressed with the results, because in 1957 the first large-scale production of ginseng was instituted in Moscow, with 60,000 plants.

Incidentally, the Soviets have also done impressive testing of another plant known as Siberian Ginseng. Botanically, it's not ginseng—it's a completely different species—but I'll discuss it in this chapter. It's widely used in the Soviet Union and it's been tested on all kinds of people, from Olympic athletes and astronauts to factory workers.

But first, back to "the real ginseng"—the one celebrated in fact and fable for so many centuries. A few years ago, I started hearing about a ginseng product that got consistently good results. The reason: this was a standardized ginseng—something that had never been available before. In the past, consumers and researchers who had tried various ginseng teas or tablets—or even pieces of ginseng root—never knew how much "effective ginseng" they were getting.

Ginseng is a plant and it's subject to the same variables as any other plant. All oranges, for instance, are not equally sweet and juicy and rich in vitamin C. The soil in which the tree was grown makes a difference. How much sunshine and rain it received affects the taste and nutritive value of the oranges. The same is true of ginseng; we can't expect every ginseng plant to have exactly the same chemical composition.

That's why ginseng had to be standardized before we could get consistent results. This new, standardized product was perfected, not in the Orient, but by the methodical and industrious Swiss. For fifteen years, a Swiss chemical company studied and experimented with varieties of ginseng from Korea, Russia, China, the U.S. and Canada to determine which was the most satisfactory plant. They also perfected a method for extracting the effective essence of ginseng—the ginsenosides. Finally they were able to produce a consistent formula. And now scientists had something reliable to test. Many studies have been conducted over the past fifteen years.

What did they reveal?

Scientific proof that the mysterious root from the Orient is a pro-oxygenator! It gets our bodies using more oxygen.

So the ancient Chinese, who believed that ginseng cured such a wide variety of problems, were not superstitious or unscientific. Oxygen affects so many processes in the body, anything that increases oxygen usage will certainly bring a vast variety of benefits.

Or it may be that ginseng affects some very basic process, and oxygenating is just one of the things that flows from that. Ginseng may be the first known adaptogen, affecting some core process in the body and therefore sending out ripples of benefits.

The Chinese probably didn't know about the importance of oxygen four thousand years ago. But they managed to send us, over the centuries, a wonderful little plant that can improve your life today. Because it can help increase your energy.

Like DMG, this standardized ginseng has shown its ability to boost physical energy, increase oxygen intake, and cut down on lactic acid after exercise. But ginseng has also demonstrated its talents in studies that test cerebral powers such as concentration and mental stamina. I'm sure these resources mean more to your career than the ability to run on a treadmill or swim an extra five laps.

One of the mental-energy tests involves watching a light that flickers on and off. You have to concentrate to distinguish between the instants of light and darkness. If you start getting tired, it becomes too much effort to keep registering the change; you start to see a steady light, even though it's still blinking.

This test is a standard measure of concentration and mental fatigue—your ability to hold your attention on one point of reality.

A group of thirty people took this flickering-light test four times during a twelve-week period. Half the people took two ginseng capsules per day. The rest took a placebo. Result: the people taking ginseng showed a 59.4 percent improvement over the twelve weeks. The placebo group improved 29.7 percent.

Another test of mind-and-muscle coordination involved following instructions and pressing the correct buttons—first with your right hand, then with your left, then with each hand alternately. It seems to me this little game would test your ability to stay focused when a lot of demands are thrown at you—just the sort of challenge you probably meet on your job.

In this test, the group taking ginseng kept improving steadily as they were tested every four weeks. In other words, four weeks of ginseng helped; eight weeks helped even more; and after twelve weeks, the ginseng group had improved 74.4 percent. The group taking placebos improved 16.6 percent.

A third ginseng test evaluated subjective things like mood and self-image. A group of sixty men and women took a series of self-assessment tests; they were asked how they felt about themselves and their lives. After taking ginseng for several weeks, the subjects said they noted an improvement in these things: attitude toward life (mood); general health; physical fitness; and the ability to get a good night's sleep. The group taking a placebo did not report these improvements.

So these test results suggest that ginseng could strengthen the powers we need in our everyday lives.

Besides these "thinking and feeling" tests, ginseng has proven its energy-boosting ability in many areas, from helping people recover faster after exercise to improving the endurance of a crack team of 450 swimming mice.

This spectacular number of aquatic mice was used to test how ginseng worked over various time periods, and whether it would build physical power progressively, the longer it's used.

Some mice took ginseng in their drinking water for fourteen days; another group for twenty-one days; and another group for twenty-eight days. Each ginseng-taking group was matched against another group that took their water straight. Sure enough, the mice that took ginseng for fourteen days did better than the mice that took none. The mice that were kept on ginseng for twenty-one days did better still. And the mice that were given the ginseng for twenty-eight days did best of all—increasing their endurance by nearly 48 percent more than the mice that drank plain drinking water.

The standardized ginseng that worked in all these tests is sold under the name Ginsana. It's made from the variety known as Korean Panax Ginseng.

One of the high-energy people you'll meet later in the book is Walter Channing, a venture capitalist, artist and triathlete. He uses Ginsana as part of his High-Oxygen Program.

So does Marilyn Grier, a computer operator and single mother of two teenagers. Besides her usual forty-hour week, Marilyn normally works a double shift once a week, from 9:30 in the morning till 1:00 or 2:00 A.M. After cabbing home to Brooklyn for some sleep, she's back at work at 9:30.

Marilyn does her own version of the High-Oxygen Program. I've never been able to persuade her to make many changes in her diet; she still eats forbidden foods like French fries and ketchup. For exercise, she goes to the Empire Roller Disco in Brooklyn on Saturday night and skates from midnight till 5:00 A.M. Or, on a Sunday afternoon, she might walk to her parents' apartment, which is more than an hour's brisk walk from her place. All of this is good oxygenating exercise.

Marilyn has a lot of energy and, with just a few changes, she'd have even more. She started taking Ginsana about two years ago. She says that when she stops taking it, she feels the difference.

Which Ginseng to Use?

Assuming you want to use ginseng, is Ginsana the only one you should buy? Or would any other Korean Panax Ginseng work as well?

Before I answer that, let's talk about another entry—a plant known as Siberian Ginseng. Most of the studies on this substance have been done in the Soviet Union; English translations are not available. However, the studies have been summarized by Bruce Halstead, M.D., a highly respected authority on Oriental medicine. Dr. Halstead went to the Soviet Union and worked with the leading Russian expert on Siberian Ginseng.

Although Siberian Ginseng is the popular name for this plant, it isn't really ginseng—it's from a completely different botanical family. Siberian Ginseng is used in the Soviet Union to increase energy and combat a wide variety of diseases. Like Ginsana, it has proven itself in "mental" tasks as well as physical. The studies Dr. Halstead describes include:

- A four-day bike race in which six of the ten top places were won by athletes who had used Siberian Ginseng.
- A study of thirty male and female Olympic runners. The athletes who took Siberian Ginseng recovered faster after exercise, had greater endurance and were ready to repeat a workout sooner than the placebo group.

The mental tests included studies in which proofreaders corrected mistakes faster and more efficiently. In sensory reaction studies, Siberian Ginseng improved the hearing of telegraph operators. Other subjects improved their night vision. A group of ship-repair mechanics, who work all day surrounded by excessive noise, were given Siberian Ginseng and experienced less hearing damage than the control group.

You can buy Siberian Ginseng in many health food stores, and it's less expensive than Korean Panax Ginseng.

So now you have three choices:

1. Ginsana, which is extracted from Korean Panax Ginseng
2. Other brands of Korean Panax Ginseng
3. Siberian Ginseng

Which should you use? The only way I could answer that would be by running tests on every brand; most manufacturers have not done tests of their own. Obviously, I can't do that. So here are the pluses and minuses of each product.

Ginsana is more expensive than some other brands. On the other hand, it's standardized—you know how much of the active ingredient (ginsenosides) you're getting in each capsule. I don't know of any other ginseng that gives this information. It may be that you would have to take more of the "other" ginsengs to get the same results you do with the standardized product.

Other Korean Panax Ginsengs use the same basic ingredient as Ginsana, and they cost less. And these brands give you the *whole* ginseng plant; Ginsana gives you just the ginsenosides. Very often, nature puts its miracles together in complicated ways. When scientists try to separate the parts, something may slip through the cracks. On the other hand, you don't know how powerful these other ginsengs are. You're not sure how much energy you're getting for your money.

Siberian Ginseng is less expensive than the Korean variety. It's been widely used in the Soviet Union for many years; so it has "consumer approval." Its efficacy is supported by thousands of tests on humans and animals. It may be a pro-oxygenator, but the studies described by Halstead don't touch on this.

How can you choose among these three?

I suggest you try one brand for four weeks, then try another. See what works for you. I can assure you that if you get a pure ginseng, you've got a natural generator of physical and mental energy. And you don't have to take my word for it. Forty centuries of Orientals can't be wrong!

8

Power Food:
How Diet Affects Oxygen
Consumption; Basic Food Rules

Are there "tiger" foods and "teddy-bear" foods?

If you didn't use caffeine—would you have more energy, or less?

Does sugar soothe or stimulate?

Or, to ask the most basic question: Is power food a scientific fact or just a wish?

It's a fact. Your diet has a great effect on your spirit, attitude and energy. But it doesn't work in the way you may think.

It's not so important that some foods give you a temporary lift. Or that there's evidence to indicate that there *are* "calming/focusing" foods and "charge-up" foods. I'll discuss these subjects more in Chapter 10. But these foods just give you a short-term fix. The most important thing you should know about food and energy is this:

Bad diet turns down the valve on your oxygen supply.

And now there's a diet that turns it up.

The High-Oxygen Diet is the one that does it, by getting your body to use more oxygen, day in, day out. That's why it's the long-term solution to your vitality problem.

If you're like most people, you're eating in a way that keeps your body and brain gasping for oxygen.

Your brain? Yes, your brain needs to "breathe deeply," too. It's impossible for an oxygen-hungry brain to create the continuous idea flow of a Thomas Edison or the spirit of an Unsinkable Molly

Brown. In other words, an oxygen-hungry brain cannot create an energetic personality.

We all know the mental affect of low oxygen. Think again of the contrast between striding along the beach, taking in all the fresh air you need . . . and sitting in a room where the windows have been closed for hours and no air is circulating. In a short time, you're sleepy and cranky, you can't think clearly; your ambition and optimism start slipping into a coma. That's how a moderate cut in oxygen affects your body, mind and personality.

A more severe shortage brings truly frightening consequences. In 1987, New York's mayor, Ed Koch, was rushed to the emergency room, suffering from nausea, dizziness and slurred speech. After a full day of tests, doctors said the mayor had suffered a momentary spasm in the brain's blood vessels. They said this had caused a slight reduction of oxygenated blood to his brain—and that's what had brought on those alarming symptoms.

What if your brain had an oxygen shortage that went on a bit longer? In just four minutes, you'd be permanently brain damaged. In six minutes, you'd be dead.

That's how important oxygen is to your brain. And it's almost as important to the rest of your body.

But, in terms of this essential nutrient, most people eat in a way that keeps the body and brain undernourished. Fortunately, *changing your diet can change the amount of oxygen you absorb.*

"Here it comes!" you say. "Another food study!" Why is it that so many of these studies end up advising you to stop eating what you like and start eating something you never heard of? You often wonder if they're making it up as they go along.

Actually, our fascination with the science of food is an old American tradition. A hundred years ago, people were debating the dangers of meat and caffeine as ardently as we are today. We just keep improving our ways of studying the questions; each generation tries new ways of approaching the problem.

One kind of research we're learning from today is the population study—we're looking at the diet habits of whole countries and ethnic groups. For instance, we've all heard about the African tribes that almost never have colon cancer—probably because they eat a lot of fiber food. Other surveys show that the Japanese have the world's lowest rate of heart disease—their diet is high in fiber, low in fat. Japan also has the world's highest rate of hypertension and stroke—they use a lot of salt. And, over the past few years, they've managed to produce their first cases of diabetes—they're learning to eat the American Way.

One very narrow-focus study compared two Swiss groups; one lived and worked in the mountains, one in town. Both groups ate high-calorie, high-fat diets. The mountain folks consumed even more fat and more calories than the townies, and they weighed a bit more; yet they had fewer heart attacks. Possible reason: they earned their living through hard physical labor, with lots of walking, climbing and carrying.

Another kind of diet research is the controlled study, in which laboratory rats or graduate students take various pills or omit certain foods from their diet or eat nothing but what the researchers give them. I read one such study with fascination and horror as it described how the graduate students not only followed the diet the lab prepared for them; they also saved their feces—neatly bagged and refrigerated—which were picked up *once a week* to be analyzed. That's dedication!

I'm discussing these different kinds of studies in order to emphasize the fact that there really is a good deal of scientific method behind all those food announcements.

Without question, the digestive process is worth the deepest study. Think about it; there's something magical about a process that turns a piece of apple pie into a human being and also supplies the energy necessary for our thoughts and feelings. Countless chemical changes are involved, and we're far from understanding them all. But every year, we discover a few more steps.

One of the most exciting things we've discovered lately is: there's a dietary way to get your body carrying more oxygen.

That's because you have to count on your blood to carry the oxygen throughout your body. And blood that's clogged with fat can't carry as much oxygen as clean, low-fat blood.

Specifically, it's the red blood cells that carry the oxygen.

Think of red blood cells as balloons that can be filled with oxygen. Each balloon should be "blown up" until it's full and round. Then it can travel through the bloodstream and deliver oxygen to every cell in the body.

Imagine a stream of these balloons traveling, one by one, through your blood vessels. That's how healthy red blood cells look when you film them through microphotography.

Now imagine that you have a lot of balloons, ready to be blown up. But first, take ten or twenty of them and pour some sticky stuff all over them; squeeze them together in your hand. Then try to blow them up.

Obviously, you can't fill these stuck-together balloons as full as you could if they were clean and separate.

Those stuck-together balloons are like red blood cells in fatty blood. They're "glued together" so they can't be completely filled with oxygen. That's one problem.

The second problem is, in order to deliver the oxygen to the cells, the balloons have to work their way through microscopically narrow tubes. A single red blood cell can slip through these tubes; a thick clump of cells can't. These clumps of red blood cells block the narrow tubes (the capillaries) so that even less oxygen gets through.

Even one fatty meal makes a difference. Hamsters who'd been rigorously following a healthy, low-fat diet and had lean, clean blood were then given a single high-fat meal. An hour later, researchers used mircophotography to film their blood. The red blood cells were clumped together. The blood was moving sluggishly through their bodies—in some vessels, the flow stopped altogether. That means less oxygen was being delivered. Later, when the hamsters' blood was cleared with a defatting drug, their blood started flowing at a normal rate again.

In another test, fourteen men were given a drink of heavy cream. A second group had no food—they fasted overnight. Sensors monitored the flow of blood to their hearts. Three hours after drinking the cream, the first group was getting 20 percent less blood (and therefore less oxygen) to their hearts than the fasting group.

Another experiment measured the oxygen reaching the brain.

In this test, cats were anesthetized and delicate sensors were placed in their brains. (I know we all hate to read about animals going through brain surgery; but experiments like these teach us something that can keep humans alive and healthy longer.)

In this test, the sensors didn't measure blood flow; they actually measured how quickly the brain was taking in oxygen. At the start of the experiment, the cats had clear, healthy blood. Later they were given a substance that makes the red blood cells stick together. Result: When the blood was thick and gluey, it took one minute longer for the brain to take in oxygen than it did when the blood was clear and normal. As you know, one minute is a very long time for your brain to be oxygen-deprived.

So these experiments and many other studies show us that there's a strong relationship between high oxygen and low blood fat, and diet. Most studies indicate that most of our calories should come from complex carbohydrates; that fruits and vegetables should be eaten raw or lightly cooked; that we need very little animal food; and that too much sugar, salt, fat and alcohol are bad for you.

Sound familiar? Yes, it turns out that the High-Oxygen Diet— the diet that's good for your energy—is the same one that's good for your heart, your liver, your colon and your weight. It makes a lot of sense; nature gave you one coordinated system. What's good for you is good for *all* of you.

I'll give you that diet in detail in Chapter 32; but I'm sure you know the basic principles. Instead of fatty meats like pork and beef, you eat more fish and skinless chicken. You skip the cheddar and cream cheese in favor of lean, light cottage cheese. You fill up on whole-grain rice, beans, pasta and cereal. And you get still more fiber from fruits and vegetables—preferably raw or lightly cooked.

One of the main diet controversies has been about how much fat you can safely eat. The guidelines issued by the federal government in 1987 say that less than 30 percent of your calories should be fat, if you're in the borderline risk group (cholesterol count 200 or higher). Needless to say, the day these guidelines were announced in the *New York Times,* an article appeared right next to it, giving dissenting opinions from other cardiologists. So if you're in a risk group, I leave it to you and your doctor to work out your diet.

While we're talking about "risk groups," let's talk about high-density lipids.

If you've been following the news on the importance of blood lipids, or blood fats, you probably know that many experts now believe that your cholesterol level is not the most important number to look at. More important is the ratio between total cholesterol and high-density lipids. Lipids and fats are not exactly the same thing; but for the sake of this discussion, I'll use the words interchangeably.

High-density lipids actually protect you from heart disease by cleaning up the blood vessels. The more HDLs you have, the more you're protected. For instance, if you have 1 milligram of HDL for every 3 milligrams of total cholesterol, you're in great shape. If your ratio is 1 HDL for every 8 milligrams of total cholesterol, you're at high risk. A reasonable, safe ratio is 4 to 1. The High-Oxygen Program is an extremely powerful tool for improving your ratio. And diet is a key part. The diet guidelines I'll give you follow the best information now available. They fit the guidelines published by the Federal government, in cooperation with such groups as the American Heart Association.

Less than 30 percent of your calories should come from fat. Another 15 percent should come from protein, and the rest—about 55 percent—from carbohydrates, mostly the complex carbohydrates.

Remember, "complex carbohydrates" are the good kind—whole wheat, brown rice, beans, fruit and some vegetables. Because they're "complex," the body has to take them apart and break them down to get at their sugar and other components. This takes time; so the sugar is fed into your system slowly.

Table sugar is a "simple carbohydrate" food. With simple carbohydrates, no breaking down is needed—the sugar shoots right into your bloodstream. Your blood sugar zooms up and then down again. This yo-yo action causes wide variations in energy and hunger levels. Complex carbohydrates don't do that.

Another good thing the complex carbohydrates do for you: because they're partially indigestible, they're less fattening. That indigestible part just exits your body without leaving a trace of weight—and it even helps clean you out as it goes.

The popularity of raw vegetables is one of the most positive food fads we've ever had. Besides their vitamins, raw foods contain enzymes that help your digestion. For instance, the enzyme in papaya is papain; commercially, it's used to make meat tenderizer. You've seen how meat tenderizer breaks the meat down, makes it softer and easier to chew. Papain does the same kind of thing when you eat it—it starts breaking down the food. All raw foods contain enzymes. They're very valuable and very fragile; just a little heat kills them. Canned foods are heated to high temperatures to destroy bacteria, including the one that causes botulism; so their enzymes are destroyed.

Eat your vegetables raw whenever possible. Start your meal with salad and keep nibbling some throughout the meal. Raw vegetables "lighten up" the main dish and help you digest heavier foods like meat, fish, rice and cooked potatoes. And raw vegetables are the ideal snack food. They're refreshing; they're not too sweet or filling.

What about meat, fish and cheese? Here's where people have really strong convictions, for and against. It's true, we can be very healthy without animal protein—we can get our protein from plant sources. But you have to be extremely knowledgeable about your selection of vegetables, if they're your only source of protein. Remember, you must choose combinations that include all eight essential amino acids. Combining rice with beans is one good way.

Vegetarians should definitely have a blood test to check their iron level; it's difficult to get enough iron on a vegetarian diet.

If you decide to eat animal protein, there are a few things to keep in mind. First, many meats and cheeses are high in fat. Stay with veal, fish, skinless poultry and cottage cheese. Pritikin's idea about cheese is a good one—use it in small amounts, as a flavoring and condiment.

In addition to being high fat, animal foods tend to be high

calorie. If you eat a lot of meat and cheese, you may not have room in the calorie budget for sufficient carbohydrates.

A third danger applies to people who try to lose weight with a high-protein diet that's also *low* in calories and carbohydrates. This kind of diet can actually deplete your muscles and leave you with a hollow, saggy look.

Digesting excessive protein is dehydrating—it pulls water and minerals out of the body. It can be hard on the kidneys; it increases uric acid and predisposes you toward kidney stones. And it can put the body into ketosis; you start burning ketones for energy and you often feel lethargic.

Bear in mind that these dangers apply to very high protein diets. You can enjoy small protions of low-fat meat, fish and cheese on the High-Oxygen Diet.

Over the past few years, you've probably been getting your diet closer to the High-Oxygen Program ideal. Maybe you still have some fatty favorites. But you've also learned some new tricks, like picking up your lunch at the salad bar instead of the hamburger hangout. Or at dinner, you choose fresh strawberries for dessert instead of cheesecake. I'm going to give you more painless tips like that. In fact, I'm going to show you how to make your very next meal more oxygenating—no matter what you eat.

Don't think these little "tricks" are unimportant. I can't over-emphasize the value of using your imagination to make your diet pleasant and convenient. This approach can mean the difference between success and failure.

In fact, many very successful "health converts" never expected to be so successful. They just took one step and enjoyed it; then they took another.

For instance, Eddie Coyle was a meat-and-potatoes man for many years. He's a sports writer on New York's *Daily News*—a morning paper—so his dinnertime can be about nine or ten in the evening. His idea of a fine meal at that hour was a huge steak with fries and plenty of beer. The worst food at the worst time!

Then Eddie got involved with animal preservation and he stopped eating meat. "I wasn't a vegetarian," he says. "I just didn't eat meat." I've seen other animal activists do that; they don't eat meat, but they still eat fatty cheese and white bread and junk food.

After being off meat for a while, Eddie started picking up nutritional knowledge, bit by bit. Now he eats a perfect High-Oxygen Diet—fresh fruits and vegetables, rice and beans and whole-grain bread. He eats eggs a few times a week because he feels that keeps him stronger.

"The extra energy was a plus," Eddie told me. "I didn't expect it. I got off meat out of respect for animals. Then, when I started eating right, I found I had a lot more energy than when I'd been eating meat."

After changing his diet and feeling more vigorous, Eddie got into a regular exercise program. Now he often runs 50 miles a week. He's 61 and plans on never retiring. Since he's a writer, he never has to.

Vegetarians are famous for living long, active lives. My friend Johnnie Lee Macfadden is 85 years old; she often works till one in the morning. Her clients are nine-to-fivers so the only way she can handle all her consultations is by working into the night and sleeping late in the morning.

Johnnie Lee is well qualified to counsel people on health and beauty. She has smoother skin than many people in their forties. She has immense energy and a sharp, fun-loving mind. She was married for many years to Bernarr Macfadden, a famous nutritionist, for over fifty years. Johnnie Lee has been on the High-Oxygen Diet virtually all her life. She loves putting together delicious meals with fruits, vegetables and nuts.

Of course, you don't have to be a vegetarian in order to be on the High-Oxygen Diet. I'm just making the point that you should make it your business to create an enjoyable diet. The more creativity you use, the less willpower you need.

That's why, besides the basic food rules in this chapter, I'm giving you just one chapter of menus—Chapter 32. Before that come three chapters on how to make good eating easy.

The "how-to-make-it-easy" chapters are:

Chapter 9. "A Fat Lover's Fantasy. How to cut down on fat

damage while you're still trying to cut down on fat." The natural food supplement discussed here also helps your body handle sugar and starch better.

Chapter 10. "Time Your Eating for More Energy." Eating the right foods at the right time makes a difference in your energy and your weight.

Chapter 11. "Noncooking Tips for Noncooks. How to make good food almost as convenient as junk food."

Then, in Chapter 32, I'll give you some menus to get you started on the High-Oxygen Diet—delicious 1,500-calories-a-day meal plans for "A Week of Great Eating." Not that you'll follow these plans exactly; I just want to show you the goal you're working toward.

Let's face it—anyone can give you "the perfect diet." Haven't a lot of people done it? I want to help you glide into that great diet. You can switch from junk food to Power Food gradually and enjoyably. That's the way to make it a permanent change.

9

A Fat-Lover's Fantasy: How to Cut Down on Fat Damage While You're Trying to Cut Down on Fat

Fat.

It sounds so bad. Why does it have to taste so good?

Let's face it, a delicious bit of fat can ruin our best intentions.

You know how it goes. You sit down to an admirable dinner of broiled fish and salad. Your potato is plain, fresh from the oven. Then you notice your teenage son's potato. He spreads soft butter on it. You watch it melt in slowly as the steam rises. Question: What do you do next?

Now it's lunchtime. You've put together an outstanding, vitamin-packed salad at the salad bar. Before closing the cover on your plastic plate, you stop to choose a dressing. Let's see—a simple wedge of lemon to squeeze over your greens? Maybe some plain vinegar? Or perhaps—just the tiniest scoop of that creamy garlic or thick, lumpy blue cheese dressing?

We're constantly struggling with these choices. For hors d'oeuvres, will you take raw broccoli, or a chunk of Camembert? On your morning cereal, will you pour skim milk or whole? Faced with a crisp brown chicken breast—will you carefully strip off the skin—or bite right into it, crunchy skin and all?

It's a fact that many foods taste better with fat. That's why we keep eating it.

Wouldn't it be wonderful if some compassionate scientist would invent a pill that allowed us to eat fat and not absorb it all? A pill that lowered our cholesterol, even though we hadn't changed our eating habits? It would be even nicer if that lovely substance would remove only the bad, harmful kind of fat (the low-density lipids) and leave us with the friendly fats—the high-density lipids, which actually protect us from heart attack.

And while they're designing this fantasy elixir, suppose it helped our blood sugar, too? We'd be much healthier if our blood sugar would stay at a steady level, instead of bopping up and down when we eat sugar and starch.

Does this sound like a pill of the distant future?

In fact, it was invented a long time ago by a kind and brilliant scientist named Mother Nature. The drug is called fruit pectin. You get some when you eat apples. Other sources are certain vegetables and citrus fruit. Or, to make sure of getting enough, you can buy apple pectin pills in the health food store.

Pectin is a fiber; we don't absorb it. Unlike wheat bran and other grain fibers, it doesn't seem to move the food through your system faster, to promote more frequent bowel movements. Different kinds of fiber have different benefits—which is why it's smart to eat both grains (for cellulose fiber) and fruits and vegetables (for pectin). Pectin does some very special things that make your diet more healthful—even if you haven't yet made a single change in what you eat.

For instance, Canadian scientists put a group of students on a totally controlled diet for seven weeks. They ate only what the laboratory prepared for them, and the researchers tried to prepare menus that were as close as possible to what the students normally ate. For the first two weeks, the subjects ate their food with no supplements. For the next three weeks, pectin was added. For another two weeks, they went back to the nonpectin diet. So there was one pectin period surrounded by two nonpectin (control) periods. For the last three days of each diet period, blood samples were taken.

Result: during the pectin period, cholesterol dropped an average of 13 percent. The decrease for individuals ranged from 5 percent to 26 percent. And this was *not* a lean diet. A day's menu for one man included butter, cheese, whole milk, ice cream and mayonnaise. The average cholesterol intake per day for all subjects was 425 mg; far higher than the under-300 mg the government recommends in their 1987 guidelines.

Incidentally, in the third diet period—when the subjects were not taking pectin—their cholesterol count went back up.

Another test, done strictly in a laboratory dish—without humans or animals—examined pectin's reaction with different *kinds* of fat. Researchers found that the pectin grabbed onto low-density lipids only; it did not touch the high-density lipids. This means pectin collars only the *bad* kind of fat and hauls it out of your bloodstream. The good fat is left to do its work—cleaning up your arteries to protect you from heart disease.

Other scientists reported the same results in tests with humans: pectin bound specifically with LDL, not with HDL.

How about pectin's effect on sugars and starches—and our blood sugar level?

Israeli scientists tested four different groups of people—diabetics, hypoglycemics, obese people and normal people. They were fed heavy carbohydrate meals (over 45 percent sugar or starch). First, they took the meals without pectin. On another day, pectin was part of the diet.

Although results varied from group to group—that is, diabetics' reactions were different from normal people's reactions—all showed an improvement in blood sugar levels; they didn't zoom up and down as much when the subjects ate pectin.

Insulin levels improved, too—they stayed steadier, longer. Here's why that's good: when your insulin rises suddenly, it eats up the blood sugar. That makes your blood sugar drop quickly. Then your energy and your mood drop, too. Very often, you want to eat more just a short time later.

Have you ever noticed that? After eating sugar, you're often hungry again in a little while. This appetite is not just psychological. Tests showed that when rabbits were forced into a sudden rise of blood sugar—by feeding them sugar—they were much hungrier a half hour later and ate twice as much as they did after a nonsugar meal. Our wonder drug, pectin, helps you avoid that sudden rise and fall in blood sugar—and the appetite that follows it.

In another study, at the Warsaw Medical School, diabetics who took pectin showed improvement in handling sugar; they also lowered their blood fats.

So here's a wonderful food that lets you enjoy a reasonable amount of meat and cheese and other tasty fats. I'm not suggesting you should pile on the butter and sour cream. The most sensible strategy is to find tricks for cutting down on fat without ruining the fun. So if a touch of butter or salad dressing makes your meal a lot tastier, go ahead and enjoy. Just take your pectin first.

How much pectin should you take? I can't give exact amounts, because not enough tests have been done on varying doses. Two 300-mg pills per meal has worked well for people I know—people who digest sugar normally. If you're diabetic or hypoglycemic, you'd need more. I can tell you that some diabetics have been able to lower their insulin doses by using pectin. *Do not* experiment with your insulin dose without consulting your doctor.

Another supplement that fights cholesterol is EPA (eicosapentanoic acid), a fish-oil derivative. It has proven very effective in lowering fats. Some people don't like the fishy aftertaste, but many find that a small price to pay.

Or, if you have a serious cholesterol problem, your doctor may prescribe niacin.

So you have a few choices. What I like about pectin is that it offers many benefits: it helps keep your blood sugar and insulin levels steady; it cuts down on "bad fat"; and it increases the ratio of "good fat" in your blood.

As you know, the level of fat in your blood has a great effect on your oxygen usage and your energy. So this completely natural food supplement is a powerful ally in your program. It's inexpensive. Taking it requires no willpower, and virtually no effort. Yet it cuts down on fat damage—and fat guilt! Pectin can be one of the first steps in your energy-building campaign.

10

Time Your Eating for More Energy

Your body has its own schedule for doing various jobs. It has natural highs and lows. Most people want a nap in the afternoon—whether or not they've had a heavy lunch. Every evening, your body temperature drops to its lowest point and you have the urge to sleep soon. Between midnight and 4:00 A.M., you create most of your new skin cells. That's why it's important to wash your face in the morning—you have to clear away the dead cells.

Biorhythms are real; but we can fight them to some extent. We do it when we work the night shift or fly across time zones. However, you'll get better results if you work *with* your biological schedule. And one of your body's important time commands is:

Space Your Eating Throughout the Day

Some people enter an endurance test every morning, to see how little they can eat during the day. Unfortunately, their evenings often become another athletic event—an eating marathon.

"Don't go out without a good breakfast!" your mother always told you.

"Don't starve yourself all day—you'll only make up for it at night," the diet gurus warn.

It makes sense, if weight loss is what you're interested in. The same number of calories, eaten in the morning, is less fattening then if eaten in the evening. And now we're discovering that meal timing affects your energy level, not just your weight.

The No Breakfast/Big Dinner routine raises your blood fats. And fatty blood carries less oxygen.

If you eat most of your food in the afternoon and evening, it's not turned into energy. During the night, it's stored as fat. Next morning, if you don't eat breakfast, your body demands some fat and sugar from its supplies. Zoom! Fat is shot into the bloodstream, where it gets the red blood cells all stuck together. Your blood starts moving slowly and glue-ily through your system, not carrying much oxygen—or energy.

But, when you eat a good breakfast—some sugar or starch, some fat and protein—the food breaks down slowly and sends a steady supply of power into your system. There's no demand for stored fuel, and no sudden rush of fat into your blood.

I'm not telling you to go to bed feeling hungry and deprived after a day's work. A light dinner can be very satisfying, when it's mostly carbohydrates. Try a big bowl of hot minestrone with a toasted bagel and a salad. Or rice and beans with tomato sauce. Or a platter of pasta, topped with steamed vegetables. This sort of meal is hot and satisfying. It helps you sleep well. And the good feeling generated isn't just psychological. Carbohydrates actually do something to your brain to turn on that contented feeling. I'll talk more about that later.

The important point for your energy is that a carbohydrate meal won't raise your cholesterol. It helps keep your blood clean—not clogged up with gobs of red blood cells.

"But I can't eat breakfast. I'm not hungry in the morning!" is the usual reason people give for their lopsided eating habits. If that's your problem, try a small experiment tonight. Eat very lightly—just a green salad or a piece of fruit. You'll be hungry tomorrow morning. Soon, your hunger pattern will change. It will be easy to eat more for breakfast and lunch, when you need the energy. In the evening, you'll feel comfortable and satisfied with light, easy-to-digest food. In fact, this is my second timing tip:

Eat Your Meat Early

Eat your meat, cheese and fish early in the day.

There are two reasons for this. Animal protein takes longer to digest. When you eat it early, the body has time to break it down and its energy is fed into your system slowly, throughout the day. Why eat that hard-to-digest food just before your body is about to switch into its rest pattern?

Another interesting reason for not eating meat at night: there's good evidence that protein is stimulating, while carbohydrates are soothing.

Upper Foods, Downer Foods

Judith Wurtman, Ph.D., a research scientist at the Massachusetts Institute of Technology, has done years of research on the effect of food on the brain. The actions of brain chemicals—some of which are food related—are incredibly complex. But Dr. Wurtman has uncovered some simple and interesting information for energy seekers.

We used to believe that we felt high after eating certain foods because they raise our blood sugar. According to Dr. Wurtman's studies, blood sugar has much less effect on our feelings than certain brain chemicals. By eating the right food, you can get the brain to produce either the "alertness" chemicals (dopamine and norepinephrine) or the "relaxing" chemical (serotonin).

Tests with laboratory animals and then with humans confirm that the right foods really do produce predictable mood changes. In the people part of the tests, subjects answered a questionnaire designed to map out their moods. Then they ate special meals. For the next three hours, they did tasks that tested their mental alertness and abilities. Every hour, they did more "mood surveys." Sure enough, both the "mood" questions and the "performance" results confirmed that some foods are soothing and others are stimulating.

Dr. Wurtman's conclusion: when you want to feel calm, more

focused and less stressed, eat carbohydrates—bagels, pasta, potatoes, corn, rice and cereal without milk. During the day, carbohydrates can help you calm down and concentrate. At night, they can help you sleep. That's because they make your blood richer in a chemical called tryptophan. Tryptophan triggers your brain to release serotonin, which is the calm-and-contented chemcial. In fact, some people buy tryptophan tablets and use them as sleeping pills. They're nonprescription and they seem safe for most people. If you take them, you may notice that you have more vivid dreams, more Technicolor dreams. You'll probably remember them better.

For alertness, Dr. Wurtman found that a few ounces of pure protein are the ticket. That means shellfish, fish, skinless chicken, veal and very lean beef.

Just a small amount of either food does the trick—3 to 4 ounces of protein or 1½ ounces of carbohydrate. Eating larger amounts does not give better results.

To get these brain-chemistry reactions, you have to eat the pure food. If you eat cereal and milk (carbohydrate plus protein and fat), you don't get the same calming effect as with plain cereal.

And remember: although a small amount of pure protein may be stimulating, a diet that's *heavy* in protein often produces a heavy, tired lethargic feeling. For steady energy, your diet should be mostly carbohydrates; that's what gives you clean blood that's rich in oxygen.

Incidentally, you may have read that meat and milk contain tryptophan; so you would expect these foods to be calming. The problem is, tryptophan is only one of several amino acids found in protein. When you eat meat or milk, all these amino acids have to compete for entrance into the brain. Tryptophan loses out. But when you eat carbohydrates, without meat, competing amino acids are moved out of the bloodstream and tryptophan has easier access into the brain. That's why carbohydrates are soothing and meat is not.

Should You Drink Caffeine?

The best answer I can give you now is: it depends.

Certainly, excessive coffee is bad for you. Aside from making you tense, it has long-term effects. For instance, one well-documented study showed that people who drink over five cups a day have more pancreatic tumors.

Some research indicates that two cups of coffee help turn your brain on in the morning. Volunteers did better on tests when they took caffeine pills than when they took placebos. The caffeine improved their reaction time and mental abilities. The pills worked for regular coffee drinkers and for people who never took caffeine in any form. Based on this evidence, it would seem that a little bit of coffee is a good thing.

However, Arnold Fox, M.D., tracked people's heart rhythms over a period of twenty-four hours and found that even two cups of coffee caused irregular patterns. Hours after the coffee drinking, the heart rhythms returned to normal.

Caffeine causes a sudden rise in blood sugar, which is followed by a fast decline. That usually means an energy drop, too. Caffeine stimulates the adrenal glands, one of the key regulators of energy. Continual stimulation of these important glands may well interfere with their normal functioning. Certainly, overuse of caffeine has its negative effects: sleeplesness, energy drops, feelings of depression. And caffeine is addictive for many people; they find it hard to keep their coffee drinking moderate.

If you can limit your caffeine to one or two cups of coffee in the morning, it may be a plus for you. On the other hand, some of the higest-energy people I know never drink caffeine. One is Henry Marsh, the Olympic runner you'll meet later in this book. Another is my friend Shirley Myers—a woman in her 50s who's hypoglycemic. Many people think hypoglycemia—low blood sugar—means low energy. Shirley plays four hours of tennis on Saturday and another four hours on Sunday, after putting in a full week's work as a stockbroker. That's because she follows the High-Oxygen Diet perfectly; and, because of her condition, she hasn't had caffeine in years.

So my answer to the question, "Should you drink coffee for energy?" is: I'll have to leave it up to you.

But to get the most vitality from your food, I can give you these three timing rules:

1. Space your calories throughout the day, starting with a good breakfast and a hearty lunch. Three meals plus a snack or two is ideal, as long as you stay within your calorie limit.

2. Eat your meat/cheese/fish early in the day; for dinner, emphasize complex carbohydrates.

3. Small amounts of pure protein may increase your alertness. A small serving of pure carbohydrate can get you calmer and more focused.

11

Noncooking Ideas for Noncooks: How to Make Good Food Almost as Convenient as Junk Food

One big reason people don't stay on a good diet is because junk foods are so available and easy to fix.

Diet books often outline excellent diets with tasty food. But I notice that virtually every meal requires real cooking and involves recipes with ten or twelve ingredients. I can't think of a single high-energy person who has the time or inclination to cook that way, except on special occasions.

Most of us are noncooks. We just toss a few things together, heat it up, and that's dinner.

So there's the solution: you've got to stock your kitchen with *good* foods that can be tossed together and heated in a few minutes. You can do it simply by putting in some time over the weekend, shopping and browsing in health food stores and supermarkets. Once you've got your staples handy, you can put together a good dinner in fifteen minutes. And you can invent meals as you go along.

The Method: A Carbohydrate Base Plus Vegetables

Your basic evening meals should be carbohydrate and vegetables—either raw or steamed. So stock up on carbohydrate "bases" that you can combine with steamed vegetables.

Here are some ideas for your supplies:

Carbohydrate bases

- Rice, pasta and beans. These are all fairly slow-cooking items, and you can't cook them in the microwave. So cook up some big batches on Saturday; divide them into portions and put each portion in a plastic sandwich bag. Then put several portions in a plastic box and freeze. Heat a portion or two, as needed, in the microwave or in a steamer basket.

- Packaged bean mix from the health food store. You'll find various mixtures—some are beans and barley; others have three or four kinds of beans.

- Canned meatless chili and canned soup.

- Falafel mix. Falafel is a Middle Eastern food made from chick peas (garbanzos) and spices. It's available in a mix—a powder you mix with water, then fry. Get it at the health food store.

Other supplies.

Buy raw vegetables once a week. Also buy some tofu, if you think you'll use it that week. Actually, tofu lasts about two weeks. It's an excellent low-fat, low-calorie vegetable protein you can use in many dishes.

Get a vegetable cooking spray, such as Pam, for low-fat frying.

Try some low-calorie salad dressings. Besides using them for salads, you can heat them up and use them as sauces for pasta and rice dishes.

Buy rice cakes and low-fat crackers.

Keep your favorite breads in the freezer—rolls, bagels, bread and muffins.

Get tahini and peanut butter, if you can use it in small amounts. If you can only eat it in gobs, keep it out of the house.

Buy plain popping corn, not the kind that's packaged with oil and salt.

Here are some examples of fast, healthful meals.

Toss-together dinners

• *Chili and vegetables* Heat canned meatless chili. For extra protein, fry tofu squares (using a vegetable cooking spray) and mix with chili. Put chopped lettuce or raw spinach with sprouts on the same dish.

• *Canned soup and warm bread.* Warm up a bagel or roll; put the soup on to heat. Steam some fresh broccoli or spinach. When the vegetable is tender, put a little steamed vegetable and hot soup in the blender, and blend to mix the flavors. Then mix that into the rest of the soup. Have bread or a bagel on the side. Add a salad.

• *Pasta primavera.* Heat up a serving of precooked pasta from the freezer. Blend it with a low-fat salad dressing. Or use tomato sauce that's made without sugar. Top the pasta with steamed vegetables.

• *Casserole.* Take a portion of rice from the freezer and put it in an individual casserole dish. Warm it up in the oven, and at the same time, steam some vegetables. When they're both hot, put the vegetables on top of the rice. Cut a slice of cheese into strips and add that to the casserole. Warm till the cheese melts.

• *Falafel and vegetables.* Fry up chunks of falafel in a pan coated with vegetable cooking spray. While it's frying, steam some vegetables. Now toss the vegetables with the falafel for a spicy, filling meal.

• *Hot and cold shrimp salad.* Although your dinners are basically carbohydrate, you can also add a little fish or poultry to your meal. For instance, steam some shrimp; toss it with a little oil and garlic. Then toss that with salad greens. Before you mix them, let the salad stand so it's not too cold. The flavors mix better if there's not such a contrast between the hot shrimp and the cold salad.

• *Stew.* Heat up a portion of mixed beans. Steam vegetables—e.g., carrots, cauliflower and zucchini—and mix with the beans.

Nibbles

If you like to munch during the evening, keep some snack foods handy.

- Break raw vegetables into a bowl and chew as needed.
- Make some popcorn, but don't add butter.
- Have a rice cake with a *thin* coat of tahini or peanut butter.
- Have some low-fat crackers.
- Mix cereal into plain yogurt.

The nice thing about "noncooking" is that it's so easy and produces such great meals, you'll find yourself thinking of new ideas as you go along. Just get started. You'll discover that good food can be as much fun as the stuff you used to like.

12

Vitamin and Mineral Checklist for Exercisers

"If you're eating properly, you don't need extra vitamins." That viewpoint, a favorite of many nutritionists, sounds sensible. On the other hand, we keep increasing our knowledge of human nutritional needs all the time. Today, we're aware of many deficiency symptoms we didn't know about ten or twenty years ago.

And when you exercise, your needs change; exercise depletes some nutrients more than others. You'll see—you start using more and more of the High-Oxygen Program and you feel a lift in energy. You get excited about doing longer, tougher workouts. You're getting strong! Then you wake up one morning with a cold or flu or just a dull, worn-out feeling. It's true, pacing yourself properly takes time and experience. But some of these "overtraining illnesses" are a result of vitamin and mineral depletion. Mineral deficiencies may be more common than vitamin deficiency.

So I recommend you take at least a basic multivitamin every day. And check to be sure you're getting the nutrients listed below, in the indicated amounts.

For most of the nutrients, I'm giving a range of requirements. One of the reasons is body size. If you weigh 105 pounds, you need less than if you weigh 185. Another reason is exercise level. Some vitamins are depleted by exercise, so you need more as you increase your workouts. For vitamin C, take a larger dosage in winter to protect against colds and viruses.

77

Vitamins

Vitamin A: 10,000–15,000 I.U. Plus beta carotene—10,000–15,000 I.U. Vitamin A is important to repair of body tissues. May offer some protection from pollution, since it protects lining of respiratory system and other mucous membranes.

Vitamin C: 3,000–6,000 mg with bioflavonoids: 1,500–3,000 mg. Vitamin C is very important in maintaining connective tissue and collagen; so it helps the body repair after injuries. Bioflavonoids help maintain veins and capillaries; may prevent varicose veins.

The need for vitamin C increases with heavy exercise and/or stress. It facilitates absorption of iron, which is necessary to oxygen transport. It's important in formation of the sterol ring from which our antistress hormones are derived—e.g., epinephrine and cortisol.

In one study, vitamin C was effective in lowering the oxygen debt. In another study, it helped red blood cells deliver oxygen to the cells more easily. (Vitamin C and the B vitamins are water soluble, and water-soluble vitamins should be taken more than once a day because we lose them in urine.)

Vitamin B_1 (thiamine): 100 mg—preferably 50 mg twice a day. B_1 is important in energy metabolism. Deficiency could limit the oxygen-carrying capacity of blood. Also necessary for carbohydrate and glucose metabolism. Takes part in the first step of the Krebs cycle, the process by which we produce aerobic energy.

Vitamin B_2 (riboflavin): 100 mg (50 mg twice a day)
Essential to the cells' oxygen transport system. Aerobic exercise burns up B_2. Sometimes, when you're training hard, you'll get a sore in the corner of the mouth. That's a sign of B_2 depletion. B_2 is found in organ meats, eggs and milk—but only in small amounts, so we don't always get enough from food. It's especially important for vegetarians to take a B_2 supplement.

Vitamin B_5 (pantothenate): 750 mg (250 mg three times a day)
Necessary to carbohydrate and fat metabolism. B_5 is a component

of royal jelly, thought to be an ergogenic (energy-boosting) food.

B_5 is essential to making the sterol ring, a building block of antistress hormones that fight infection and help combat stress. Although vigorous exercise is good for us, it's also a form of stress.

Folic acid: 400–800 mcg

Folic acid is a B vitamin that's important in protein metabolism and red blood cell formation. Deficiency can affect oxygen transport. You should be tested twice a year for your folate (folic acid) level and B_{12} level.

You can get a type of anemia from folate deficiency, and that affects energy.

Niacin B_3 (niacinamide): 100 mg (50 mg twice a day)

Necessary for glucose and fat synthesis and for the tissue's use of oxygen. One study indicates that niacin has an ergogenic effect during anaerobic exercise. Sprinters improved their times significantly when taking niacin. But don't take niacin just before long-distance runs. It decreases fatty acids fifteen to thirty minutes after you take it. Fatty acids help you produce energy for aerobic activity.

Vitamin B_6 (pyridoxine): 50 mg twice a day for exercisers; 25 mg twice a day for nonexercisers

Necessary for carbohydrate, fat and protein metabolism. Important in formation of red blood cells, which carry oxygen. Helps in breakdown of glycogen; so it probably helps in endurance activities. Also helps premenstrual women with water-retention problem.

Vitamin B_{12}: 1,000–2,000 mcg once a day

Essential for normal formation of blood cells. Necessary for carbohydrate, fat and protein metabolism. Is considered ergogenic. Check your B_{12} level once a year, especially if you're a vegetarian. This checkup is important, even if you're a meat-eater, since you may have absorption problems.

Vitamin D: 800–1,000 I.U.

Supplementation is necessary only if you don't eat dairy foods. Vitamin D is necessary for absorption and utilization of calcium and phosphorus, which are required for formation of bones and for neural transmission. Necessary for normal muscle contraction—both the heart muscle and the skeletal muscles.

Vitamin E: 400–800 I.U. of d-alpha tocopheryl

Important for all exercisers, and especially during a long workout. After thirty minutes of exercise, we burn fatty acids instead of glucose. Vitamin E protects the fatty acids so that they're available for energy production. In one study, vitamin E was given to subjects tested at an altitude of 5,000 to 15,000 feet. Results: The vitamin E group increased their oxygen usage (VO_2 MAX.) The placebo group did not get this result.

Minerals

Potassium and sodium: The checkup you get before you start exercising should include tests to determine your baseline electrolytes—sodium, potassium, chloride—and CO_2. That will indicate your requirements. Usually, in a multivitamin, there's enough potassium—99 mg—and we get plenty of sodium in our diet.

After heavy sweating, some replacement of electrolytes is warranted. Many athletes are interested in electrolyte drinks, such as ERG and Gatorade. Actually, replacing the water is more essential than replacing the electrolytes, except for very heavy exercisers like marathoners.

Magnesium—half your calcium dosage (see below).

Magnesium is lost in sweat, so exercisers must replace it. It's necessary in over one hundred reactions in the cell. Magnesium deficiency seems to be related to seizures. Heavy exercise can bring on seizures in people who are predisposed to them; this may be due to a magnesium deficiency.

Calcium: 1,500 mg for men and premenopausal women; 2,000 mg for postmenopausal women.

Important for maintenance of bones and teeth; muscle contraction; neural transmission; immune system.

Iron: I prefer not to suggest the amount of iron you should take because people vary in the amount of iron they absorb. Have iron studies when you're starting your program. If your doctor recommends supplementation, the studies will be repeated three months later.

Iron is a constituent of oxygen-transport compounds in the blood and cells. Heavy exercisers need more iron due to excessive loss in sweat. Also, red blood cells are damaged by the pounding of the feet in running. Anemia impairs the blood's ability to transport oxygen.

Chromium: 100 mcg in the form of GTF or brewer's yeast. Important for heavy exercisers. Helps in glucose metabolism. We don't absorb all the chromium we take in, but the dosage given allows for that fact. Important for heavy exercisers and people who drink tea or coffee—coffee and tea deplete chromium.

Selenium: 150 mcg (50 mcg 3 times a day)
Take selenium with vitamin E. It's an antistress nutrient and aids the healing process. Found in broccoli, cabbage and organ meats.

Zinc: 150 mg (50 mg 3 times a day)
Stimulates the immune system. Important to wound healing. Little white dots under the fingernails indicate zinc deficiency.

Copper: 2 mg
Trace element. Works with vitamin C to form elastin. Found in whole-grain foods, leafy vegetables, beans.

Iodine: 15 mcg (2 kelp tablets)
Influences speed of metabolism because it affects the functioning of the thyroid gland.

13

The Rats That Grew Bigger Brains: How Exercise Transforms Your Chemistry to Boost Your Energy and Brain Power

Read these statements:

"You go without me; I don't feel like it."

"It's not worth the effort."

"It'll never work out."

Who's the author of those words—a tired body? Or a depressed mind?

It's hard to say which comes first, because both the body and the brain can get low in energy.

Fortunately, exercise works on both areas. I'm sure you've noticed that people with a lot of physical drive also have a lot of mental stamina. Problems don't look as tough to them; they see the world differently from "tired" folks.

For the past ten years, we've been reading about how exercise remodels the body—how it makes your heart larger and your blood pressure lower. That it not only widens your blood vessels, allowing easier blood transport; it even makes you grow *new* blood vessels. Exercise actually works right down to the cellular level. It makes your cells grow extra "energy generators" (mitochondria).

Those are some of the physical effects of exercise.

Exercise also changes your *brain* chemistry.

You already know that your brain needs plenty of oxygen to function at its best; naturally, oxygenating exercise makes a great difference. And you've heard about endorphins—the "natural opiates" that seem to be released by exercise.

But there's another brain chemical that's affected by exercise— a substance called NE (norepinephrine). NE is a "messenger chemcial" the brain needs to send information from one nerve to another. Your NE level influences how low or lively you feel. With manic depressives, the level of NE in the blood is much higher during a manic stage. It drops drastically during the depressive stage. Aerobic exercise causes a moderate increase in the amount of NE in your bloodstream.

If you exercise more than thirty minutes, your adrenal glands also release endorphins and adrenaline (epinephrine).

So doing oxygenating exercise is like giving yourself a shot of a drug that affects motivation, aggressiveness and optimism.

That's one big reason why so many people have become "exercise freaks"—it really does make you feel happier. This has been demonstrated many times in controlled studies.

In one of these, conducted by Robert Dustman, Ph.D., two groups of older people (aged 55 to 70) followed different exercise programs for four months. Tests showed that the people who did *aerobic* exercise improved their reasoning power, memory, reaction time and mental flexibility.

The second group—people who did exercise that was *not* aerobic—did not get the same benefits.

What is aerobic exercise? It's exercise that forces more oxygen through your system; usually, it makes you huff and puff. But it must be easy enough so that you can keep doing it for a long enough time. Starting and stopping weakens the effect.

Anaerobic (nonoxygenating) exercise is exercise that doesn't keep you breathing hard for a long time—for instance, weight lifting, or a tennis match consisting of brief spurts of running interrupted by strolls from one side of the court to the other.

In the study with older people that I mentioned, one group did vigorous long-distance walking (aerobic); the other did stretching and strengthening exercises (anaerobic.) With this second group, the instructors made sure the subjects' heart rates did not reach their "exercise levels." I'll explain that later. The point is, your heart has to be beating hard enough to pump more blood through your system than when you're resting or strolling. The people who increased their oxygen intake through aerobic exercise got far greater mental and physical benefits than the other group.

Another test of the happy-making power of oxygenating exercise was done by John Greist, M.D., director of the psychiatric clinic at the University of Wisconsin.

Patients who described themselves as depressed were divided into two groups. One group received traditional "talking" therapy; another group simply jogged regularly.

At the beginning and end of the study, the subjects answered a list of questions about their feelings. Based on their answers, they were scored for degree of depression. At the end of ten weeks, the group that received traditional therapy averaged a two—"a little depressed." The jogging group scored a zero—not depressed at all!

And, in rats at least, exercise has even changed the size and structure of the brain.

In one laboratory, rats were given housing that forced them to live inactive lives. A second group was given a rodent health club— stairs to climb, treadmills to run on. The second group were not only physically healthier; they actually grew larger forebrains and more complex nerve structures than their sedentary neighbors.

Frankly, information like this gets my attention. We've all seen "Bionic Woman" and "Bionic Man" stories on TV. Someone is transformed—maybe by accidental exposure to radiation—and suddenly, the working of their brain is radically changed. Their body chemistry is altered, too. From that moment on, they have superhuman powers of mind and body.

I think of aerobic exercise as a "bionic transformer." I continue to be awed by my friends and patients who dramatically increase their life power as they increase their exercise.

Laura Madson started running when she was 25. Gradually, she got onto the High-Oxygen Diet. Then she got interested in biking. Then she added swimming.

Now she's 33. She runs 10 miles a week and rides a bike about 100 miles a week. Every morning at 5:30 she swims a mile. During the eight years that she was building up her exercise schedule, she got her MBA at night, sometimes going to school four nights a week. During the day, she pursued a demanding career in computer sales. Recently, she moved to California—in large part, because it's easier to do outdoor exercise there. In California, she's looking forward to a long season of triathlons—as she builds her position in her new job at AT&T.

"Forget it!" you say. "I'm not the superjock type!" Maybe you imagine that some people came into the world with the words "Born to Exercise!" tattooed on their chest. Not true.

Ed Coplon started running because he loves to eat and he was getting fat. He says eating is still one of his major motivations for exercising.

According to Ed, "I woke up one morning when I was about 38 and weighed 185 pounds; I'm 5'8"." Since he has a family and an active career as an architect, he started running just a few miles a week. Then a few more. And he made some changes in his diet.

"Eventually, I lost 35 pounds. By that time, I was hooked on running."

Now Ed is 48. He still loves to eat, but he's pretty solid on the High-Oxygen Diet. He eats dessert only if it's really worthwhile. He runs about 45 miles a week. His business is in the suburbs, about an hour from his home in Manhattan. Many nights, he's in a local town meeting with community planning boards till one or two in the morning.

Besides his running and career activities, Ed recently designed and built his weekend home on Long Island, and he and his wife had a second child. (Their firstborn is 12 years old.) Having the new baby meant they had to move into a bigger apartment. And while all this was going on, Ed also became president of the Central Park Track Club.

So exercise can definitely transform your life. But you don't have to follow a schedule like Laura's or Ed's. You can give yourself the gift of more vitality in just five sessions a week. These five workouts—totaling two and a half hours—can change the chemistry of your brain and body.

In fact, exercise is the most important way of achieving the basic goal of your energy program, which is increasing your oxygen usage. Here's how you get started:

1. Get a medical OK.
2. Find out how hard you should exercise.
3. Start easy, three days a week.
4. Aim for an exercise program of five days a week—three days of hard exercise, two days easy.
5. Have an alternate program in mind, for weeks when you're too busy to do the full program—or just don't feel like it.

Step 1. Get a medical checkup. This is essential at any age. If you're over 35, I recommend a stress test.

I know you think a checkup is important for other people but not for you. However, very few people who get heart attacks are expecting them. They usually think they're doing fine. Sometimes, they're people who exercise regularly and feel sure they don't have a problem.

Step 2. Find out how hard you should exercise. There's an easy way to do it. Just check the column of the Exercising Heart Rate chart on page 90. Let's say you're 30. The chart tells you that your exercising heart rate is 152.

Now start exercising. After a few minutes, stop and count your pulse for ten seconds. Then multiply by six.

If after a few minutes' exercise, your pulse is 160, you're exercising too fast; slow down a little. If your pulse is under 152, speed up the pace of your exercise.

Let me add a "but wait" to what I just said. The chart gives your correct rate *if* your resting heart rate is average. That's about 72 beats per minute for men and 80 for women. If your resting heart rate is faster or slower than average, use this formula to calculate your exercising heart rate:

$$\frac{(\text{Maximum Rate} - \text{Resting Heart Rate}) \times 65\%}{+ \ \text{Resting Heart Rate}}$$

Exercising Heart Rate

Notice that the formula starts with a number called "Maximum Rate." You'll find that on the chart, too. Your maximum rate is the fastest speed at which your heart can beat, no matter what you do. It's related to your age.

The next number you need is your resting heart rate. The best time to take your resting heart rate is before you get out of bed in the morning. If you want to take it during the day, first lie down and rest for fifteen minutes.

When you're taking your pulse, there are two places where you can easily feel your heart beating. One is on the inside of your wrist. Hold the inside of your right thumb with the two middle fingers of your left hand. Run those two fingers down your thumb, down the pad below your thumb, and stop at your wrist. You'll feel your pulse there.

Another easy spot is the hollow of your neck. Put a finger (not your thumb) in the hollow of your throat and you'll feel your pulse.

Step 3. Choose your sport and start easy. Cross-country skiing, running and swimming are the best oxygenating sports. That's because you need a sport that gets your heart beating hard enough and *keeps* it beating steadily. The exercises mentioned fit that bill— they keep you moving at a regular pace, for a long time.

Biking can be good, if you keep working hard enough. But remember that it's easy to cruise and relax when you're biking. Rowing is very good; you're using your arms, and that picks up your heartbeat. Jumping rope and jumping jacks are fine—if you can keep a steady pace. Walking is good, but only if you do it fast enough. The same goes for roller-skating and ice-skating. If they're too leisurely, they're not doing you much good. So remember to keep checking your heart rate.

Start your exercising habit by working out for fifteen minutes, at your proper pace.

Let's say you're using a stationary exercise bike, or you're doing some aerobic dancing. Exercise comfortably for a while; just enjoy yourself. After a few minutes, count your pulse for ten seconds. If you're below your exercising heart rate, speed up if you want to. But don't push. You may not be able to work out a full fifteen minutes at your exercising rate—not if you haven't been active until now.

The important thing is to build a habit of working out for fifteen minutes. After three or four weeks, more of your time will be spent at your full speed.

Most likely you'll start strong, with lots of enthusiasm. In the first or second week, you may start feeling tired during the day. Then you wonder if the exercise is draining your energy instead of building it. What you should do is get to bed a bit earlier at night, or take naps, if you can. Even a fifteen-minute nap helps a lot. Keep exercising your full fifteen minutes, but at a very slow, easy rate. Building your habit is the important thing now—doing some sort of workout, three times a week.

Step 4. Reaching your exercise goal. As you go along, you'll want to spend more and more of your fifteen minutes at your full exercising rate. Gradually increase workout to twenty minutes and then thirty. Your final goal: thirty minutes of exercise three days a week; fifteen minutes of exercise two days a week.

Each time you increase your effort, you'll probably feel a little tired. But after it's happened a few times, you'll know the tiredness will pass. You'll look forward to feeling a new level of strength and enthusiasm in everything you do.

Step 5. Supporting your exercise habit. Just when you think you've finally transformed yourself into a human dynamo, you'll hit a week when you don't want to do those five workouts. You're too busy, either with work or weddings or bar mitzvahs. Or you just feel annoyed and fed up; you don't feel like changing into your running clothes when you get home from the office.

Now you may skip your workouts. So what? Missing one week certainly won't hurt you.

The strange thing is, it's very easy to lose that good habit of exercising. When you're into it, you love your biking or swimming time. You look forward to it; you know you could never live without this happy time in your day.

But somehow, you skip a day here and a week there. Then you realize that you haven't exercised in three weeks and you haven't even missed it. Now you have to go through the slow process of getting back in the groove.

A much better system is to have an "easy-week" plan—something to do that's a whole lot better than nothing. For instance, your "easy" program can be fifteen minutes of exercise, three times a week. If you can't fit it in any other way, do it at lunchtime. Find an empty office or conference room. Close the door and take off your shoes, if you wear heels. Now do jogging in place or jumping jacks or dance steps. When you're finished, you'll feel alive and invigorated; and more important, you won't have broken your habit. The next week, you can swing back into your regular routine.

What you'll discover is that exercise doesn't cut into your life; it helps you do more than you ever thought you could.

Carol Hudson started running when she was 30. Now she's 45, and she's doing far more than she did fifteen years ago. And, she says, "I *feel* like doing more. I don't feel like lounging out. I walk or bike almost everywhere I go; I never take buses or cabs."

Carol is a vice president of Healthtex clothing company, where she's responsible for three separate clothing lines, from design to marketing. She runs 40 miles a week. She's in a biking club and edits the club newsletter. She often combines her two sports. For instance, if there's a race in Rockland County, which is 28 miles away, she and her friends will bike there, run a 6-mile race, then bike back.

Again, you don't have to follow that kind of routine. Carol does it because she likes it.

But exercise is not optional. It's one of the basics of staying alive and healthy. It keeps your heart beating. It helps keep your bones from thinning in osteoporosis. It's proven itself as a successful therapy for depression and other emotional problems.

Once you get started, you won't exercise to avoid illness. You'll do it because exercise is one of the strongest forces in your life for keeping you alive and winning.

Recommended Heart Rate During Exercise

Age	Exercising Heart Rate	Maximum Heart Rate
20	160	200
22	158	198
24	157	196
26	155	194
28	154	192
30	152	190
32	151	189
34	150	187
36	149	186
38	147	184
40	146	182
45	143	179
50	140	175
55	137	171
60	128	160
65+	120	150

14

Instant-Energy Breathing:
An Ancient Yoga Technique

When you're feeling sleepy, low or foggy brained, do the following breathing exercise. It will lift your energy immediately.

1. Sit up straight. Breathe with quick, panting breaths. Only your belly should move, not your chest. Take twenty to thirty of these quick panting breaths.

2. Fill your lungs with air. Let your lungs expand. Hold for the count of 50 or 60.

3. Exhale fully. Press your belly in, to put some pressure on the lungs and squeeze out as much air as possible.

Repeat 3–5 times.

During the fast-breathing part of this exercise, you'll start feeling more stimulated. The sleepy feeling starts breaking up.

The second part—when you hold in the air—gives the blood in your lungs time to absorb as much oxygen as possible. Some people feel a tingling in their skin at this time. Yogis describe the breath-holding part as a time to "store energy"—to increase your body's reserves of oxygen.

You can do this breathing exercise wherever you are, any time you need a quick energy lift.

If possible, get up and move around after the instant energy breathing. If you're at work, take a walk down the hall, as quickly as possible. Even better: close your office door and do jumping jacks.

Any vigorous movement—like fast walking or jumping—does two things for you: you breathe hard, so you get more oxygen into the body; and you pump your blood faster, so the oxygen is delivered faster. When you see your face turn pink during exercise, you know you're sending more oxygen-rich blood to the skin—and to the rest of your body.

Yoga teaches that the life force—*prana*—is found in the air. People who are very experienced in yoga breathing techniques stay healthy on less food. They've learned to extract more energy from the air.

Your Style of Breathing Makes a Difference

Yogis have studied the body's reactions for centuries. They teach that some methods of breathing are stimulating; some are soothing; some are cleansing. You've observed for yourself that different breathing techniques affect you in different ways. For instance:

Shallow breathing. You do this when you're scared. You're tense, so you tighten up your muscles and hold on to your breath instead of letting it flow in and out.

You've heard the expression, "We waited with bated breath." "Bated" means the same as "abated"—stopped or reduced. When we hold or diminish our breathing, we decrease our oxygen supply. This lowers our energy and keeps us from thinking as clearly as we need to in an emergency.

Taking one good deep breath. We do this to relax at the end of a tense moment, especially if we've been "holding our breath" for a while. The tension is over, so now we inhale a lot of oxygen and then release it. We get the energy flowing naturally again.

When you feel yourself holding your breath from tension, take one deep, relaxing breath. Next, pay attention to your breathing to be sure you maintain a natural pace—not holding, not panting. If it's hard to get that natural pace started, do a few "relaxing" breaths: inhale for the count of eight, hold for the count of eight, exhale for the count of eight.

Hyperventilating. This is excessively fast and deep breathing that causes decreased levels of carbon dioxide. People sometimes do it when they're very anxious. When you hyperventilate, the blood vessels in the brain tighten up, and that produces faintness, tingling of the fingers and toes and even loss of consciousness. If you realize that you, or someone else, is hyperventilating, the solution is to breathe into a paper bag. This gets the carbon dioxide recirculating in your body.

Breathing is a reflection of your physical and mental state. It's a crucial part of our health, a way of getting continual nourishment. Yet we pay very little attention to it. Any time you're anxious or tired or tense, take a moment to notice your breathing. Get it going in a calm, steady flow and you'll feel your whole body respond and relax.

Eating, Drinking and Inhaling Fatigue

I'm going to assume you're really serious about conquering your weary, draggy feelings; so serious you're tough enough to take the meanest words a person can say to you: "You're doing it to yourself!"

The fact is, a lot of fatigue is caused by things you put into your body every day. Sugar and drugs—including tobacco, caffeine and alcohol—can be a continual drag on your vitality.

You can read about the pros and cons of caffeine in Chapter 8. The other energy-killing substances are discussed in the following four chapters.

I can't tell you it's easy to break any of these habits. But I can tell you that getting rid of these substances can lift your spirits and your stamina more effectively than you can imagine. Just by *not* using an energy killer, you're taking a big step toward becoming the clearheaded, lively person you want to be.

15

Sugar

"You know what Frank Shorter ate before he won the Olympic Marathon?"

"Sure!" (Chomp, chomp) "Chocolate chip cookies!"

That was a popular conversation about ten years ago, when the fitness boom was just getting started. It was a favorite excuse for sugar addicts.

In fact, people who've just started exercising are often hit with a strong sugar craving. And sometimes they can get away with it; they can eat sweets and not gain weight. This happens to people who increase their exercise drastically in a fairly short time.

But we've all learned that sugar causes energy drops. Do exercisers get away with that too? Or does the ice-cream cone you grab after your workout cause a tired feeling later? It's hard to tell, because when you're just getting into exercise, you often *do* have low moments in the day. You're still getting used to spending a lot of energy.

We all know why sugar causes energy drops. You feel tired, so you take something sweet to boost your blood sugar. The sudden rise in blood sugar stimulates a release of insulin, which quickly lowers the blood sugar; then you feel low again.

Although we've all experienced this sugar reaction, Americans still eat tremendous amounts of sweets. Every year, another sugar franchise crops up—ice-cream stores, frozen-yogurt stores, David's and Famous Amos and Mrs. Fields cookie stores. Even popcorn—a good, whole-grain food—is sold with a variety of sugar coatings.

It's true you can "get away with" eating a little sugar, especially if you exercise a lot. But if you feel a real need for it and you're eating candy or cookies three times a day, that's a danger sign you shouldn't ignore. It may be just a bad habit right now; sugar can get you in its grip very easily. Break it before you create a real malfunctioning in your body—hypoglycemia, which can become diabetes.

Since the taste for refined sugar is learned, you can unlearn it. There's enough natural sugar in fruit, vegetables and grains to satisfy your appetite. And it's the kind that's released slowly, so it doesn't jangle your sugar-control mechanism or your energy level.

As the healthy life becomes a habit, you'll discover that you're stronger and healthier with no refined sugar. You learn that it's normal to feel tired occasionally; you don't have to fight it with cookies. You can use instant-energy breathing to give yourself a lift; you can close your office door and do a few minutes' jumping jacks. Or you can just wait. You'll liven up again.

Sugar is an essential element in a healthy life, but if you misuse it, it can be a killer. Keep your body supplied with the natural sweetener you get in food. That's the kind of sugar that keeps your body and brain functioning at their highest level.

16

Tobacco

If you smoke, I know very well that you want to quit. So I won't focus on the negative; you already know that smoking keeps your energy down. What I want to do is give you three pieces of good news:

1. Even while you're still smoking, you can limit the damage.
2. When you quit, your body starts repairing itself almost immediately. Your energy picks up very rapidly.
3. You *can* quit.

Swedish scientists kept track of men who'd had one heart attack. Some of the men quit smoking after their illness; some didn't. Those who quit had half the death rate of those who continued. And the longer you stay stopped, the closer your risk of heart attack approaches that of someone who has never smoked.

"But I've failed so many times!" you say. So have a lot of successful quitters. A huge percentage of them tried many times before they finally made it.

How to Start Getting Healthier While You're Still Smoking

• Take plenty of vitamin C; every cigarette inactivates 25 mg of vitamin C. I can always tell when a new patient is a smoker;

his or her skin is more wrinkled than it should be for their age. Vitamin C is important in the formation of new collagen, which maintains firm, smooth skin. The amount of vitamin C recommended for exercisers—3,000–6,000 mg with half as much bioflavonoids— is a good amount for smokers to take.

• Take beta carotene to reduce the risk of cancer. Beta carotene is a precursor of vitamin A, and tests have shown that it helps prevent cancer. You can get beta carotene by eating plenty of carrots, cauliflower, broccoli, spinach, cabbage, sweet potatoes and cantaloupe. And you can buy a bottle of beta carotene pills in the health food store. If I were a smoker, I'd take 50,000 mg a day.

You've probably read that too much vitamin A causes liver damage. The damage is usually done by vitamin A derived from animal sources. Beta carotene doesn't have the same danger of toxicity. But if you're taking a lot of vitamin A *or* a lot of beta carotene, have your liver function tested every three months.

• Cut down on the number of cigarettes you smoke. Look at your smoking habits and identify some cigarettes in your day that you can live without. Not only will this make it easier when you finally stop; it also cuts down on the damage cigarettes are doing to you. In Australia, researchers at the Human Morphology Unit of Flinders University examined structural changes in the lining of smokers' lungs and airways. Former smokers had less damage than current smokers. And the degree of abnormality was directly related to the total number of cigarettes the people had smoked. Any cigarette you can cut out is helping you.

Besides, you'll feel happier about yourself; you know you're not a helpless victim. You're fighting back. Slowly, your unconscious will get used to the idea that you're not a smoker.

• Switch to a brand with the lowest tar and nicotine content.

• Start doing aerobic exercise. Even if you do only fifteen minutes a day on a stationary bike, or take an aerobics class three times a week, you'll be pumping more oxygen through your body, and this boosts your energy and spirits.

Of course, you understand why smoking cuts down on your energy—the key to energy is high oxygen usage. And no one has to tell you that smoking interferes with oxygen usage. You're constantly getting messages from your own system: your breathing apparatus feels clogged; you're the first one to catch any flu that's going around; and you feel winded after climbing a flight of stairs.

As uncomfortable as all these signals are, there's more going on that you don't feel. Smoking is silently changing your blood chemistry. Smokers tend to have lower levels of HDLs (high-density lipids)—the "good fats" that help keep your blood clean. If you have a low level of HDLs, your blood is thick with harmful fats; and that means it's carrying less oxygen. So, even when some oxygen *does* get through your clogged lungs and into the bloodstream, your blood can't carry it all—so it isn't turned into energy.

I'm not telling you this to make you feel worse, but just to point out that you can help yourself by exercising now. Aerobic exercise *increases* your HDL at the same time that it's forcing more oxygen through your lungs.

You'll even notice your spirits improve when you start exercising. This isn't just psychological; there's a basic physical reason for your mood lift.

For one thing, smokers get less blood and less oxygen to the brain, and that's depressing. In a study at the Veterans Administration Hospital in Houston, blood flow to the brain was measured. Smokers' brains were getting much less nourishment than nonsmokers'. (This is possibly why smokers are five times more susceptible to stroke.) Exercise dilates your arteries, allowing more blood to flow through. So when you get into oxygenating exercise, you're sending your brain more oxygen—more of what it needs to create clear thoughts and positive feelings.

Aerobic exercise also stimulates your brain to release endorphins, the natural "feel-good" chemicals. Incidentally, there's some evidence that *smoking* releases endorphins too. So when you stop smoking, you're probably withdrawing from those pleasurable endorphins, as well as nicotine. Aerobic exercise is a direct and positive way to get the endorphins going again.

In fact, regular exercise builds such good feelings, I'm tempted to say that if you build your exercise habit, you'll automatically lose your smoking habit. You start feeling so alive and vigorous that the cigarettes feel more and more unnatural. They're not "you" anymore.

And your health improves each time you work out. When you huff and puff, you're getting rid of carbon dioxide, along with other poisons. You'll probably cough and expectorate as you run or ride your bike. That's good—it's the body's way of tossing out the garbage.

How to Succeed at Getting Rid of Cigarettes for Good

I know; you've tried ten times and you always went back to smoking. Go for it again! The eleventh time may work.

Sometimes, enough of a scare can do it. My friend Judith Griffin had gone on and off cigarettes many times. She finally stayed stopped when she saw a woman in her office dying of lung cancer—and still refusing to quit.

Another patient, Peter Bergstein, paid to get scared at the Petrie hypnotherapy organization. They showed the group films on how smoking can kill you. Then the leader of the seminar dumped a pile of black, stinking ashes on the table, to illustrate how much you're taking in, in a lifetime of smoking. After group hypnosis, each person was given a hypnotic tape to play once a day. That was fifteen years ago, and Peter hasn't smoked since.

Hypnosis can help; it can make your life easier while you're quitting. But don't expect it to be a magic wand. A spokesperson for the American Board of Psychological Hypnosis reported only 30 percent success using hypnosis alone. You should plan on combining hypnosis with behavior modification, exercise and mutual-support groups. Use anything that will get you through.

Here's a diet trick that can help: for the first weeks off cigarettes, avoid alcohol and cut down on meat. Eat plenty of fruit, nuts, seeds and vegetables. This diet keeps your system alkaline and keeps you from releasing the nicotine from your body too quickly. You'll feel less withdrawal misery if the nicotine leaves your body gradually. If you have withdrawal symptoms, it often helps to take

Alka-Seltzer Gold. Those symptoms are often a sign of hyperacidity.

You should also consider using a nicotine gum. It's a prescription drug. In a British study, 47 percent of the people who used it were still free of cigarettes one year later. People who used a placebo gum had only 21 percent success at the end of the year.

Some people think the gum is a bad idea, since you're still taking nicotine. But at least you're not putting all that smoke and tar into your lungs. There's something to be said for breaking one habit at a time: first, the smoking habit, then the nicotine.

Another study showed less weight gain among people who used nicotine chewing gum—probably because they didn't feel such sudden deprivation. Again, this gum is not magic; you should still use exercise and behavior modification and everything else to help you through.

Speaking of weight gain, don't use that as a reason for not stopping. Smoking is a greater risk to your health than obesity. A man between the ages of 45 and 74 who smokes a pack a day has a 64 percent greater risk of heart attack than a nonsmoker. A person who's 30 pounds overweight has a 22 percent greater risk than a slim person.

Okay, let's say you've started your exercise program. You've cut some cigarettes out of your day. You're feeling better and you're ready to get rid of this habit once and for all.

Plan your attack intelligently. Choose your time to stop. Set a date, about one week away. During that week, make smoking less comfortable for yourself; start breaking some of the sub-habits.

Switch to a brand you don't like. Throw out any cartons you may have.

Make your cigarettes harder to get to—put them in a plastic bag and wrap a rubber band around it. Keep a pencil and paper in the same bag. Before you light up, write down the time of day; keep track of how many cigarettes you're smoking. If you can cut down some more during this last week of smoking, that will give you a feeling of success and excitement about getting rid of them altogether.

You might want to see your doctor and get a prescription for nicotine gum.

When your Stop Day comes, make it as easy as possible. Many experts recommend making it a nonworking day—it's less stressful. Don't be alone; line up a friend to spend time with. Do some exercise—a long, brisk walk or bike ride—and feel the air filling your lungs. Congratulate yourself. You're great, praise yourself! Enjoy the "up" moments of the day. Later, if there's a certain hour when you're very used to smoking, and you're afraid you'll miss that cigarette, plan to be at a movie or concert. That will keep you clean for a few hours.

Plan your second day to be a lot like the first. Exercise, be with friends, organize distracting activities. On the physical level, these two days are the worst.

Now you've got to get through your first working day. Use substitutes for the many sub-habits of smoking. Put a plastic cigarette in your mouth. Get a Rubik's Cube or worry beads to keep your hands occupied. Chew sugarless gum or carrot sticks.

Use self-hypnosis to keep from getting too tense.

Here's an easy hypnotic technique. With your eyes open, roll your eyes up. This is a strain; it makes you want to close your eyes. Take a few slow deep breaths, then let your eyes close. You'll feel very relaxed. Now give yourself positive suggestions. See yourself running on the beach. Feel your lungs fill up with clean healthy air. Your lungs are now cleaning out the dirt and poison with every breath. Your eyes look clear, your skin is fresher because you're free of toxins. You're stronger, you're full of energy and you have such wonderful self-confidence because you've gotten rid of this horrible burden that's been slowing down your life. You now have the optimism and power to make your life whatever you want it to be!

Use this relaxation technique several times during the day. Just three or four minutes spent on these positive images can make the difference between success and failure, because they keep the tension from building up.

Incidentally, if you have trouble sleeping these first nights, take some tryptophan tablets. Once you're through the hard part, sleep will come easier. Nicotine can interfere with good sleep. Researchers found that nonsmokers fell asleep in about thirty minutes, but smokers lay awake for about forty-five minutes. Heavy smokers who quit decreased their stay-awake time by 45 percent, in just the first three nights.

When you're through your third day, you'll feel very encouraged, but still not secure. Good. Stay on your guard. Keep using every technique that helps.

After a week, you'll be feeling better and you may start letting your guard down. Or you may lose sight of your goal; the struggle seems too hard. Give yourself a reward—radio earphones to wear while jogging or tickets to a show. Just get through the second week. Most failures happen between the seventh and tenth days. Remind yourself of your great victory in getting through Week One. Trick yourself into staying clean: make a resolution to stay with it for fifteen minutes. Then do it another fifteen minutes. You'll get through the day.

Be ready with some instant techniques for fighting the urge:

Self-hypnosis or a hypnotic tape.

A mini exercise session. Find a place where you can jump up and down for three to five minutes. Get your blood pumping and the oxygen rushing through your body.

Aversion therapy. In one stop-smoking clinic, they teach this method for fighting the urge. Take smoke into your mouth and hold it for thirty seconds. Focus on the unpleasant sensation, the terrible taste in your mouth. The clinics that teach this technique say it has doubled their success rates.

This is an aversion therapy that's safe. You may have heard about another one that's not: rapid smoking. Rapid smoking makes you nauseated and dizzy. It's dangerous for people with heart disease.

And here's a long-term technique:

Mutual help groups. Many people with years of success give credit to their group. You may be amazed to find how long it takes to get over the emotional problems you've swallowed down, along with the smoke. Weeks and months after the physical addiction is gone, former smokers find themselves "going crazy." The most common problem is anger. Your group can help you accept your anger and express it in constructive ways.

And it probably helps to see people who are "newer" than you. If you've been off cigarettes for a month, maybe it's still not easy. But you see someone suffering through the second or third day, and you feel better. You realize you'll never, never have to go through *that* misery again.

No, it's not easy to stop smoking. But you can do it. If you don't adopt any other energy-building idea in this book, do this one. Conquering this addiction can open the door to energy, accomplishment and good feelings you never knew you had. Discovering them—discovering *yourself*—is part of the adventure.

17

Alcohol:
Where Does Alcohol Fit into the High-Energy Life?

Alcohol has a lot of high-powered language attached to it. "High proof" sounds like "high octane." We talk about "tanking up," as if we were taking in fuel. Kickapoo Joy Juice, the Dogpatch favorite, sounds like it would give you a lift. Even words like "punch" and "spirits" suggest strength. And everyone knows it takes a strong man to hold strong liquor.

Well, what about it? Is alcohol a good drink for dynamic people?

Some high-powered people do drink a lot. They work nonstop, they can't leave a job unfinished; they're perfectionists about their careers, their sports, their children. In other words, many energetic people are compulsive. They don't know how to relax. Someone like this is a natural for excessive drinking. "I work hard, play hard and drink hard!"

Maybe you can work hard, play hard and drink hard when you're 20. But your body isn't built to take that kind of treatment for many decades.

People who want a long productive life usually decide to drink moderately or not at all.

But which is better?

That's a difficult question to answer. Alcohol is a lot like caffeine. Both are drugs. Both are harmful in excess, but may be helpful in moderation. And different people have different sensitivities to them. One person's "moderate amount" makes another person depressed or overanimated or belligerent.

One fact to keep in mind: alcohol is a depressant, like Valium and barbiturates. It affects the frontal area of the brain first—the control center for civilized function and inhibitions. When your inhibitions are depressed, you feel exhilarated for a while.

If you keep drinking, the alcohol starts depressing the more primitive parts of the brain. Your memory is affected, then your muscular control. You start getting numb. Finally, you stop breathing.

As I'm writing this, there's a story in the news about a Rutgers student who died after one drinking session, at a fraternity initiation. It can happen.

Alcohol's depressive action suppresses the adrenal glands' response, so it can calm jittery nerves. That's helpful in competitions requiring calmness and control. One event in the Pentathlon is shooting; steadiness and control are important. Naturally, it's illegal for an Olympic competitor to have alcohol in his blood.

Even if you drink moderately, bear in mind that you're drinking a depressant, so it's liable to make you sleepy, slow and moody. Many high achievers don't drink at lunchtime because they don't want to slow themselves down.

What about dinnertime? Wouldn't that be the best time for a drink? Your working day is over and you don't mind an energy drop.

That's true; but evening drinking can affect tomorrow's energy. You know how it works—you drink a bit too much; next morning, you're dull and draggy. Sometimes, the lowered feelings are with you all day. Just two glasses of wine at dinner make a difference for some people. Next morning, they don't have their usual bounce. It takes them a bit longer to get the motor turning over.

So if you like to start your day with a run or a workout at the gym, or if you just want to get into the office early and get a jump on the day, you may decide that even moderate drinking is working against you.

This is the conclusion I've reached for myself. Growing up in Kentucky, I always assumed that hard liquor was a normal part of having fun. In college, our official fraternity drink was truly homegrown—200-proof moonshine, manufactured by my fraternity brothers from Eastern Kentucky. We used this elegant product to make Blue Blazers: you fill a shot glass with liquor, set fire to it, then blow out the flame and toss it down. Any 19-year-old who downs a few of these just *knows* he's a tough hombre.

But as time went on, I realized that I could accomplish my athletic and career goals much more easily without the help of Kentucky corn liquor. So I decided that total abstinence is the answer for me. I love waking up with a totally clear head. When I go out for my morning run, I like knowing I haven't slowed myself down to the slightest degree, even by taking a few beers the night before. And I like knowing that my head will still be clear in the evening, if my wife and I are going to the theater, or if I just want to do some reading or writing. Getting rid of alcohol has added hours and energy to my day.

But this is a question you'll have to explore for yourself.

Can alcohol boost your engery, or improve your health in general?

You've probably heard that moderate drinkers have fewer heart attacks than teetotalers. Some studies have shown that moderate drinkers have higher levels of "good" blood fats than nondrinkers—the high-density lipids that prevent clogged arteries. But these studies prompted a question: Maybe moderate drinkers tend to be healthy people who exercise? If so, it could be the exercise that was raising the HDLs, not the three beers.

Researchers at Baylor College of Medicine in Houston set up an experiment involving men of various levels of physical activity. Some were marathon runners; some were joggers; some did no regular exercise. For twenty-one days, all the subjects abstained from alcohol. For the next twenty-one days, they all drank three beers a day.

Results: the alcohol had no effect on the HDL level of the marathoners and joggers. During the nondrinking period, their HDL level didn't change. During the drinking period, it didn't change. For the nonexercising group, moderate alcohol *did* raise the HDL level. But their HDL levels were still 16 percent lower than the exercising groups.

And even that 16 percent increase should be questioned now;

lately, we've learned more about these lipids. Lipids are not pure fat; if they were, they wouldn't mix easily with blood. High-density lipids are fat with a protein coating (actually, protein, cholesterol and lecithin). So when scientists used to say that "alcohol increases the amount of HDL in the blood," they were mistaken. What they were measuring was the *coating* that might later pick up fat and become HDL. This "pre-HDL" coating has been dubbed HDL-3. The "real" HDL is HDL-2. As of this writing, we don't know if that alcohol-inspired coating, HDL-3, ever does become the good stuff—HDL-2. But, the HDL you create when you jog is the genuine article—the powerful cleaner that clears the fat from your arteries and protects you from heart disease.

But what about all those studies in which moderate drinkers had fewer heart attacks than nondrinkers?

To begin with, it's almost impossible to measure all the lifestyle differences of the people questioned in these studies. Maybe moderate drinkers are more relaxed, sociable people than teetotalers. Someone who drinks a single glass of wine with dinner sounds like an orderly, well-balanced person who has his life in order. Or maybe nondrinkers have some inherent physical weakness that makes them oversensitive to alcohol—and that's why they don't drink. Some of these studies include sober alcoholics among the "nondrinkers." These people may have damaged their hearts during their previous years of excessive drinking.

Or we may find out that a little alcohol *is* good for your heart.

On the other hand, moderate drinking has some clear negatives, like increased risk of stroke. According to the National Heart, Lung and Blood Institute, light drinkers—people who have two or three drinks a day—had twice the risk of stroke as nondrinkers. Heavy drinkers had almost three times the risk. This fits with alcohol's tendency to raise blood pressure. If you're a man over 50, drinking affects you like excess poundage. It raises your systolic blood pressure as much as a 30-pound increase in weight. Women over 50 run a similar risk, if they're not taking estrogen.

Drinking before exercise in the cold weather is dangerous, since it can lead to excessive heat loss. This can lower your total body temperature and cause frostbite.

These are some risks associated with moderate drinking. I don't have to tell you about the damage done by excessive drinking. It can destroy the liver, the most important filter in the body. Your liver is responsible for keeping your system from being poisoned by the countless harmful substances we take in, in modern life.

Heavy drinking is linked with increased risk of cancer of the mouth, larynx, esophagus and respiratory tract. It affects your brain. Alcohol interferes with the oxygen supply to the frontal lobes, the thinking brain. After one year of excessive drinking, the brain can suffer visible deterioration.

And binge drinking is highly related to fatal heart attacks. In fact, British researchers who examined coroners' reports on one hundred sudden deaths found that nearly 25 percent of the fatalities happened shortly after the person had drunk alcohol.

But that's heavy drinking. Until all the facts are in, we can probably conclude that moderate drinking is acceptable in a high-achieving lifestyle. It can help you relax without sapping your energy, if you use it properly.

The next question is: What is "moderate" drinking? And are you an alcohol-sensitive person—someone who shouldn't drink at all?

Definitions vary, even among scientists who study alcohol's effects. Most authorities say a moderate drinker does not drink every day; three or four days a week is usually considered okay. Moderate drinkers don't spend more than an hour or two drinking. So if you go to a party that lasts four hours, you would spend part of that time drinking club soda. If you're a 150-pound man and you were only drinking for one hour, you could have two drinks of hard liquor at 1.25 ounces per drink. The equivalent in beer is two 12-ounce glasses; in wine, two 4-ounce glasses.

A moderate drinker might overdo it two or three times a year. But usually, he or she finds it natural and easy to stay with small amounts.

But there are some people who are sensitive to alcohol, just as some people are sensitive to caffeine and sugar. For them, even small amounts bring adverse effects.

If you have extreme reactions to alcohol—personality changes or blacking out (forgetting what you did while drinking), you're probably sensitive to it. If you notice you need more liquor to get the same effect you used to get—in other words, if you're building up a tolerance—that's a sign of sensitivity. Daily drinking—even if the amount is moderate—can be a sign. If one of your parents is alcoholic, you've got a better chance of being one, too. You might want to discuss the question with your family physician.

The organization that's most experienced with problem drinking is Alcoholics Anonymous. They've worked out a twelve-question quiz to help you evaluate your drinking. You'll find it at the end of this chapter.

If, after honest observation of your habits, you decide you can drink safely, you may still decide not to drink at all. Many ambitious people make that choice and are very happy with it. They find there simply isn't enough time in the day for a career and family and exercise and cultural pleasures—and drinking, too. On the other hand, if you're a high achiever—if you're intense and energetic—a few drinks a week may be good for you. It could give you a chance to slow down and see the world from another perspective.

This is your choice. And it's a very important one. The right decision can mean the difference between just getting through life, and living the full, joyous life you were born for.

How Do You Know Your Drinking Is a Problem?
Twelve Questions to Help You Decide

Alcoholics Anonymous has over fifty years of success in helping people who are not happy about their drinking. They stress self-evaluation and self-help within a very practical program. Here are the twelve questions they've found useful to people who are examining their drinking pattern.

1. Have you ever decided to stop drinking for a week or so, but only lasted for a couple of days?
2. Do you wish people would mind their own business about your drinking—stop telling you what to do?
3. Have you ever switched from one kind of drink to another in the hope that this would keep you from getting drunk?

4. Have you had to have an eye-opener upon awakening during the past year?
5. Do you envy people who can drink without getting into trouble?
6. Have you had problems connected with drinking during the past year?
7. Has your drinking caused trouble at home?
8. Do you ever try to get "extra" drinks at a party because you do not get enough?
9. Do you tell yourself you can stop drinking any time you want to, even though you keep getting drunk when you don't mean to?
10. Have you missed days of work or school because of drinking?
11. Do you have "blackouts"? (Hours or days you can't remember, even though you were conscious.)
12. Have you ever felt that your life would be better if you did not drink?

If you've answered "yes" to four of these questions, you should drop in on an AA meeting and listen to how other people have handled their drinking. The meetings are truly anonymous; no one will ask your last name and no one will pressure you into joining. After you listen awhile, you may decide your drinking is perfectly normal and healthy. But, if you have any question, it's certainly worth an hour of your time to listen to some people who no longer have a problem with alcohol.

18

Cocaine and Amphetamines

The stimulant drug of the sixties was amphetamines, just as today's is cocaine. While cocaine is known as a high-roller's drug because it's so expensive, amphetamines affected many more people in a very short time.

Amphetamines were legal then, inexpensive and easily available. Thirteen-year-olds were given prescriptions by diet doctors. Jet-setters got shots from Dr. Feelgoods. College students and house-wives popped pills to keep themselves working without much sleep.

It took a number of years before people realized that "uppers" were dangerous drugs. The end of the sixties saw the first street campaign against drugs; lapel buttons and bumper stickers spread the "Speed Kills" message.

Today, the overdose deaths of sports heroes are alerting young people to the unglamorous side of cocaine. And the testimony of athletes and film stars is letting us know the habit can be kicked.

The two drugs do similar things to your body. Both cocaine and amphetamines get the brain to release one of your natural "energy chemicals," NE (norepinephrine), until your supply of NE is depleted. That's one of the reasons for the "crash"—the exhaustion and depression that follow stimulant use.

Both stimulants mask the effects of fatigue—they don't actually create new energy. And they interfere with the body's fatigue alarm system; you don't know you're exhausted until you collapse.

After a crash, the user has to sleep for hours. Then he wakes up feeling tired and depressed, so he takes more speed or cocaine.

Both drugs stimulate the central nervous system and the heart. That's why they cause trembly hands, headaches, flushed skin, rapid heart rate with irregular beat. High dosages can cause cerebral hemorrhages and coma.

Psychological effects are similar, too. The user becomes excitable, anxious and confused; he finds it hard to distinguish between reality and fantasy. Eventually, addicts become paranoid and grandiose.

When they withdraw, they're tired, disoriented and depressed.

If you're taking a stimulant, your doctor can guide you to a treatment program. Treatment in many rehabilitation centers is covered by health insurance. And some people can withdraw without going away to a rehab. Your doctor's supervision and a local out-patient program may be all you need.

Even if you don't think you're addicted, see your doctor and get some help before the problem gets worse. I know it isn't easy to admit you're concerned about a possible drug habit. If it's any help, just remember that this is an extremely common situation these days; you won't be the first person who's talked to your doctor about drugs. And once you get involved in a therapy program, you'll find lots of good company. People who've been off mood-changers for a while will show you that the straight life can be exciting and fulfilling.

Diane Hawkins is a model/actress/dancer who's also getting her degree in nutrition. Her recreation is running ultra marathons—usually, races of 50 miles and more. For the past two years, she's been the top woman ultra-marathoner in New York. In one twenty-four hour race, in Houston, she had just passed her 100-mile mark when she had to stop because a tornado blew away the tent holding her food and supplies. "It was just like the Wizard of Oz!" she said.

Not a very dull life!

And Diane—a former amphetamine user—does it all without so much as a cup of caffeine in the morning. "Now my energy comes from wanting to accomplish a lot in life and from enjoying what I'm doing," she says. She finds that having multiple careers actually decreases the pressure. "In the acting field there are a lot of disappointments. After an audition, you can sit home waiting for the phone to ring. Instead, I go right out for a run after an audition and I enjoy myself. Then if I get the job, it's a bonus." She enjoys waking up in the morning with a variety of things to look forward to—running, acting, college classes, shooting a commercial.

People often take stimulants because they want to feel superhuman—brilliant, powerful, tireless. Instead, they're dragged into extremes of nervous excitement, frightening fantasies and depression that finally end in psychosis or death. It's an existence that's quite a bit less than human.

And that's why more and more people are learning to live without stimulants. They're finding that ordinary human life can be pretty terrific.

Sick and Tired:
Six Fatigue Diseases

You may have opened this book, not because you need a little energy boost, but because you're abnormally, deep-down tired. If you never feel quite healthy and energetic; if life hasn't seemed worth the effort for a long time; if your fatigue doesn't go away after a restful weekend—you may need medical help.

You can't diagnose your own illness, but the following brief descriptions will give you some insight into the most common fatigue diseases.

19

Anemia

"Iron-Poor Blood!"

That catchphrase sold a lot of iron supplement in the thirties and forties. The ads featured drawings of sad, pale people, so tired they couldn't stand up straight. The campaign disappeared as the government tightened its regulations on health claims in advertising. But the fact is, iron-deficiency anemia does cause fatigue. And even in our prosperous country, many people—chiefly women and children—don't get enough iron. Even if you don't have anemia, a slight deficit in iron can leave you feeling tired and low.

How do you know if you're anemic? You should suspect it if you look pale and feel weak and tired. You might feel close to fainting at times. And you might have heart palpitations—you can feel your heart beating quickly; it's pumping faster, trying to get more oxygen through your system.

Why does lack of iron make you tired? It goes back to the basis of the High-Oxygen Program. Iron is an essential part of hemoglobin, a protein in red blood cells that combines with oxygen. So you need iron to carry oxygen, and if you don't have enough iron, you don't have enough oxygen—or energy.

You can store iron in the body—you keep your extra supplies in the bone marrow, ready for emergencies—so you won't normally run low, unless you lose blood. You may sustain blood loss due to injury or surgery. Otherwise, for men, it's rare, although it can happen when a man has bleeding ulcers or hemorrhoids.

But for women, before menopause, regular blood loss is normal. That's why menstruating women are susceptible to iron-deficiency anemia. Their Recommended Daily Requirement (RDA) is 18 mg of iron per day, and many women don't get that much. A man's requirement is only 10 mg per day, and that's not hard to fill.

But many people are on iron-deficient diets. If you're cutting calories and your menu consists mostly of foods like cottage cheese, yogurt, lettuce and fruit juice, you're not getting enough iron. Iron-rich foods include liver, roast beef, lean ground beef, turkey dark meat and white-meat chicken. Vegetarians can suffer from iron-deficiency because the iron in fruit and vegetables is not the kind we absorb easily. So if you're a vegetarian and you're exercising a lot, it's important to have your hemoglobin checked regularly.

Even if you're eating liver and broccoli three times a week, you should know that some foods keep you from absorbing iron. Coffee and tea contain tannin, which can block absorption of 40 to 50 percent of the iron in your food. So it's better not to have these drinks with meals. Even necessary substances—calcium and vitamin E—block iron absorption. If you take those calcium supplements, take them on an empty stomach, not with food.

But lack of iron in your diet is not the only reason for anemia. Lack of B_{12} or folic acid can cause it. Or you may have a disease in which there is excessive destruction of the red blood cells (hemolytic anemia). Another anemia is the sickle-cell type; it's a genetic disease in which abnormal red blood cells are produced.

Whatever the cause, if you suspect anemia, don't try to cure it with self-prescribed liver and iron pills. You may bring about some improvement without really bringing your iron level up to par. Or you may be masking another form of anemia. See your doctor for a blood test. He or she may prescribe an iron supplement; then your blood will be monitored, to be sure the correct iron level is maintained. You'll need regular checkups for a while, but it's worth it. Your blood is your power line. You've got to get it in shape so it can do its job—carrying the oxygen you need to keep your whole body healthy and vital.

20
Low Blood Sugar

Some people say hypoglycemia—low blood sugar—isn't even a disease. It's a normal reaction to refined sugar.

However you choose to think of it, hypoglycemia is a condition in which your body overreacts to sugar and refined starch (simple carbohydrates). Normally, when you eat sugar, your blood sugar rises a little. Then it falls a bit, as the food is digested.

If you're hypoglycemic, simple carbohydrates make your blood sugar zoom up. Then your pancreas overreacts—it sends out a burst of insulin to cope with the sugar. Now your blood sugar plunges down and you feel low-blood-sugar symptoms again; you may feel dizzy, anxious, confused and trembly.

If your blood sugar is very low, your adrenal glands get into the act. They try to help by releasing adrenaline, which raises the blood sugar level. Now you feel "wired"; you're into the "fight or flight" reaction.

All this overreaction eventually tires out both your adrenal glands and your pancreas. The pancreas can become too tired to produce enough hormones; then you become diabetic.

You should suspect hypoglycemia if you have frequent sugar cravings and the ups and downs just described. Hypoglycemics often feel like they're having an anxiety attack. You might have cold sweats and lowered body temperature. You might feel your heart pounding rapidly. You might have headaches.

The most reliable test of hypoglycemia is the six-hour glucose tolerance test. After fasting, your blood sugar level is measured. Then you drink a specific amount of glucose. Over the next six hours, your blood sugar is taken several times. If it falls below the fasting level, you're considered hypoglycemic.

The treatment is exercise, diet, and food supplements.

Exercise. Oxygenating exercise helps your body handle sugar more efficiently. In fact, diabetics who exercise live longer than those who don't. So the exercise that's recommended for normal people is a lifesaver for hypoglycemics and diabetics.

Diet. The diet for hypoglycemics has been a subject for debate over the past ten years. Years ago, you would have been advised to eat lots of protein and very little carbohydrates. When more was learned about the dangers of excess protein and the value of carbohydrates, some nutritionists went to the other extreme. They recommended virtually no animal protein.

But many hypoglycemics do well on the basic High-Oxygen Diet outlined in this book. You emphasize grains, beans, vegetables and fruit, and you take a small amount of animal protein—meat, fish, cheese or yogurt. A protein snack at bedtime can prevent low blood sugar in the morning. Plain yogurt with a little cereal in it is great.

While proper diet is important for everyone, it's essential for hypoglycemics. You *must* eliminate sugar, refined carbohydrates, caffeine, and alcohol. Other people may have a little leeway with these substances; but you can go into a low-blood-sugar attack after a candy bar or a cup of coffee.

Supplements. Supplements can do a lot to get you in balance. B vitamins are essential. So is chromium; take it in the form of GTF (Glucose Tolerance Factor) or brewer's yeast. Chromium helps your body use insulin more efficiently, so your blood sugar curve stays smoother.

Another excellent supplement is pectin. Many tests have shown that pectin keeps the blood sugar level more stable, even with sugar and starch meals. This is not to say that the subjects showed normal reactions; but their blood sugar and insulin levels didn't vary so much. If you're hypoglycemic, talk to your doctor about taking a couple of pectin tablets with every meal.

One of the advantages of being hypoglycemic is that you're forced to live a good life. You've got to be on a perfect diet and you've got to exercise. You get instant biofeedback if you don't live right.

I have a hypoglycemic friend who sometimes "treats himself" to a cup of coffee. Within fifteen minutes, he's sweating and trembling.

And I've seen others who make me say, "I can't believe you're hypoglycemic"—because they have such exceptional energy.

If you're hypoglycemic, you can still be one of the toughest competitors on the track. Low blood sugar does *not* have to mean low energy—it's all up to you.

21

Underactive Thyroid (Hypothyroidism)

Years ago, you'd sometimes be able to see an underactive thyroid. It was a bulge in the neck called a goiter. Today, you virtually never see an enlarged thyroid.

This doesn't mean the problem has disappeared; it's been estimated that ten million Americans have underactive thyroids. But they don't have the iodine lack that causes the thyroid to enlarge.

Here's how that works. In order to make its hormone, thyroxine, the thyroid needs iodine. If it doesn't have enough iodine in its cells, it creates more cells, striving to get more iodine. That's why an iodine deficiency can cause an enlarged thyroid. A nondrug cure for hypothyroidism is kelp, because it contains iodine.

But if you've got the problem, you'll notice other symptoms long before your thyroid is noticeably enlarged. If you're tired, maybe depressed; if you're physically colder than other people; if you have trouble losing weight, you should suspect an underactive thyroid.

Other symptoms and signs are dry skin, coarse hair, high cholesterol and a gritty feeling to your eyes in the morning. Older people are more likely to have underactive thyroids than younger people. Women have underactive thyroids more often then men; one of their symptoms is an unusually heavy menstrual flow.

The thyroid regulates how quickly you create energy. To put it another way, it regulates your metabolic rate. If it's overactive, you feel like you're running in high gear. If it's underactive, you feel like you don't have enough juice.

Because the thyroid is related to energy creation, it affects your temperature, your weight and your fatigue level. You can see how that works: If you're not burning fuel fast enough, you're cold, tired and overweight. The unused fuel is stored as fat.

There's a test you can do yourself, if you suspect a problem. Take your underarm temperature first thing in the morning, before you get out of bed. Put the thermometer under your arm and rest a few minutes. Normal temperature is 97.0 to 97.5 degrees. If your temperature is low, that's an indication of an underactive thyroid.

The diagnosis and treatment are fairly simple. Your doctor will test your blood for free thyroxine and other factors. If your levels are abnormal, you'll probably be given a low dose of thyroxine and be tested again in a few weeks.

Even if your blood count is in the low-normal range, your physician will probably let you try thyroxine and see if you feel any better. The onset of hypothyroidism is subtle and gradual; so your reaction to the therapy is an important indicator.

If you continue on the medication, your feelings of coldness and fatigue will clear up. Unfortunately, I can't promise a fast weight loss. You'll have to work on that the usual way—with good diet and exercise.

22

Allergies

Allergies have always been a mystery, because you can be allergic to virtually anything, from the living-room rug to invisible particles of petroleum in the air. So pinpointing your allergens has always been a job. Now, it's tougher than ever.

For one thing, we're just learning about the effect of food allergies. For another, it's likely that more people are becoming allergic or "sensitive" or "intolerant" to more things.

We're increasingly exposed to unnatural materials like plastic; and to other materials that are natural, but hard to live with. Examples are lead and arsenic and petroleum wastes.

Some of these substances are actually inhaled into the body. Others are rejected; but that's extra work for the immune system.

So that's two strains on your body: foreign materials that upset your chemistry; and an overworked immune system. Under this double strain, some people start having bad reactions to ordinary stimuli, such as pets and foods.

Whether you're allergic to food or to something in the environment, start being very aware of your symptoms and when they occur.

Environmental allergies. Notice when and where your symptoms are worst. If you feel terrible in the morning and start getting better after you get to work, the culprit may be the down in your pillow or something else in the house. See if you react more in one room than another. Perfume is a common irritant; notice if you start sneezing around perfume or cosmetics. Start making a list of suspect substances and then see an allergist. He or she can help you identify your problem. But many allergists are not very aware of food allergies.

Food allergies. By "food allergy" I don't mean simply breaking out in a rash from strawberries or having your throat swell up after eating shellfish. As dangerous as that symptom is, it's still very obvious. And you can identify the cause readily.

The "mystery" food allergy is the one that makes you tired, depressed and anxious. Tiredness is a very common symptom of food allergy, and people can suffer from it a long time before they realize it has anything to do with something they ate. The reaction can come hours after eating, so it's hard to relate the two events.

And food sensitivity can cause symptoms that feel like other illnesses. For instance, you may drag around for months, thinking you have some kind of flu—you're not exactly sick but not really healthy. Or you might be dead tired at eight in the evening, every evening. Or you might have headaches several times a week. Other symptoms are depression, anxiety and mood swings—reactions often related to low blood sugar.

At least 140 foods have been reported in clinical literature as proven allergens. The most common culprits are the foods we eat a lot of. In this country, that's wheat, milk, corn and eggs.

Usually, a food allergy is the last thing you think of when you're feeling sick. But if you're habitually tired and your doctor hasn't been able to find a reason, you might want to try an elimination diet.

For three days, eat only the foods that are least likely to cause bad reactions: green and yellow vegetables, poultry and fish (but not lobster; many people are allergic to lobster). If your tiredness or headache or other symptoms go away in those three days, you can start looking for the guilty food. The do-it-yourself way is to start adding back one food at a time. One day, eat something made with corn. If you're still okay, have a milk food the next day. The next day, try something made with wheat.

When you start looking for professional help, be sure the doctor you choose has experience with food allergies; many allergists don't.

The most reliable test for food sensitivity is the RAST test (radioallergosorbent). It measures your immune system's response to a particular substance.

Solving your allergy problem can take time. Especially with food allergies, you need a lot of patience and motivation. First, you have to eliminate each food entirely; then even when you can eat a food, you may not be able to have it every day. For a while, planning your meals is a complicated process; it absorbs all your attention. But stick with your diet.

Eventually, your "rules" become automatic. And you'll be happy to see that you can tolerate more and more foods. You get very used to the fact that some foods are on your "almost never" list. After a while, your diet becomes easy and habitual. And best of all, your energy is back, you're not stuck with headaches and mood swings; you feel like a normal person again!

23

Mononucleosis and Chronic Mono (Epstein-Barr Virus)

If you had to pick a disease by its nickname, these two would be big favorites.

One is known as the kissing disease.

The other is the yuppie's disease.

They're both debilitating illnesses that leave you physically weary and mentally depressed. You're unable to handle your usual job, much less exercise or have a social life. And they have no simple cure.

Aside from their deceptively appealing nicknames, the two conditions seem to be true relatives with the same parent—the Epstein-Barr virus, a herpes virus. It was named after the doctor who discovered it.

Mononucleosis is called the "kissing disease" because it can be spread by mouth and it's often contacted during the college years, when students have contact with a lot of new people.

The symptoms may vary from person to person; but they often include sore throat, inflamed tonsils, sore and swollen glands—especially in the neck, armpits and groin. The patient may have fever, aching joints and skin rash. As the disease progresses, he becomes extremely tired, both mentally and physically. He may feel depressed for months after the infection has cleared up.

If you have these symptoms, your doctor will order a blood test for antibodies that are typical during mononucleosis infection.

The treatment is bed rest; and that's all you'll feel like doing.

Your doctor may prescribe large doses of vitamin C to strengthen the immune system and the liver. The virus usually invades the liver, and vitamin C is very effective at rejuvenating this organ. You'll probably be given aspirin to lower your fever.

Virologists estimate that nearly everyone is exposed to the Epstein-Barr virus by the time they reach adulthood. Yet most of us don't succumb. Susceptibility is probably related to the effectiveness of the immune system; so the best way to protect yourself is to keep your immune system strong with plenty of exercise and supplements, such as vitamins C, A, E, and selenium, zinc and DMG.

Mononucleosis is a tough disease to get through. But at least people do recover. Another disease—which seems to be a relative—is much worse. It's called Chronic Epstein-Barr Virus because it's believed to be caused by the same organism. So far, no true cure has been found. People just have to learn to live with it.

CEBV is known as the yuppie's disease because it often strikes intelligent, ambitious young people who live active, stressful lives. Far more women then men succumb to this virus.

It's also called chronic mono because the symptoms are just like those of mononucleosis: fatigue, aching joints, sore throat, swollen glands. The immune system is weak, so patients are susceptible to allergies. And there are mental symptoms: mental lapses, inability to concentrate, depression.

Diagnosis includes testing for Epstein-Barr antibodies; but many experts believe the cause isn't simply the virus. The real culprit may be environmental toxins that reduce our immunity to the virus.

There's been some success in treating CEBV with oral acyclovir, a drug used for reducing the symptoms of genital herpes.

But for the most part, people simply learn to live with it. Basic good health habits are the best treatment. Intravenous vitamin C drips are used to stimulate the immune system.

Because patients don't fully recover their energy and can't cope with a demanding job, they often have to switch from a high-pressured field to something less stressful. Although a career change can be traumatic, the person eventually feels stronger and more positive after he or she has done it. People feel less stress and more energy when they're in control of their job.

People with CEBV have formed national mutual-help groups. Members learn to cut down on stress and activity; they try to get the most out of life, even though they have a lot less energy to give.

24

Candidiasis
(*Candida albicans* Infection)

Having candidiasis is a lot like having food allergies.

Both problems are progressive—more and more substances make you sick. Both are hard to diagnose. Both have mental symptoms; you yourself wonder if your problems are psychological. And if you have candidiasis, you probably do have food intolerances.

Candidiasis is a chronic infection by a yeastlike fungus called *Candida albicans*. We all have it in our bodies. If the fungus is confined to the intestines or vagina, it's not much of a problem. But if it penetrates into the tissues, the fungal products get into the bloodstream and can affect many physical functions.

Some of the physical symptoms are lack of energy, headaches, dry scaly skin and acne. You may have abnormally frequent urination, and burning when you urinate. You may have either diarrhea or constipation; and you start having bad reactions to various foods. You may be allergic to synthetic fabrics.

Some of the symptoms are mental. That doesn't mean they're "psychological," that is, emotionally caused. The fungus can affect the brain as a physical organ, just as allergies and low blood sugar do. It has nothing to do with neurosis.

What I'm saying is, suppose you have hypoglycemia, low blood sugar. Your brain will be deprived of its fuel, sugar. So you'll become confused, unable to concentrate, maybe tearful.

These are not signs of emotional disturbance. They're signs of a physical organ that's low on fuel.

The same sort of thing happens with candidiasis. The patient may have headaches, fatigue, depression, loss of ability to concentrate, loss of memory. She may feel "spacy" or "foggy." Naturally enough, she wonders if "something is bothering her"—something in her emotional life. The same question occurs to her physician. And since this is a difficult disease to diagnose, many patients are told that their problems are psychosomatic.

I'm referring to the patient as "she" because candidiasis affects women more often than men—usually women between the ages of puberty and menopause.

This problem is usually treated by an internist. Before you see the physician, ask him if he's done much work with candidiasis; not many doctors have had experience with it.

The diagnosis involves both blood testing and a trial treatment period.

Your doctor will do some oral, rectal and vaginal cultures and possibly blood cultures. Sometimes the physician will test your blood for antibodies to the fungus. He'll ask about the history of your symptoms, how they've changed over time. He'll ask you about yeast-promoting factors. For instance, antibiotics and birth control pills promote the growth of yeast. So do immune-suppressing drugs.

If you've had a vaginal yeast infection recently or frequently, that's a clue.

If your physician suspects candidiasis, he or she will start treating you for it, just to see how you respond. If some of your symptoms respond within the first few weeks, the doctor will assume you have candidiasis and will continue the treatment.

You'll take a fungicide called Nystatin. This is a drug that's been used for over thirty years and has proven its safety.

Your diet will be changed; you'll have to eliminate food that promotes the growth of yeast. This means starch and sugar and foods containing mold, like cheese, mushrooms and vinegar.

You'll eliminate birth control pills. Progesterone seems to favor the growth of yeast.

The object of treatment is to eradicate the fungus enough so that your immune system can take over and fight it. The immune system is strengthened with vitamin C, preferably intravenous. And you're given candida vaccine, to stimulate your response to it.

Treatment can take several months. It's hard on the patient, because usually you've been getting progressively sicker, more tired and more depressed for a few years. You've gone to more than one doctor and you're frustrated at their inability to find the cause and cure. You've probably been told that it's all a neurotic condition.

When you finally establish that you have candidiasis, you're at a low ebb, physically and emotionally. You may have to continue working if you're self-employed or if your company doesn't have long-term illness benefits. At the same time, you have to follow a restricted diet—not just to eliminate starch, but to eliminate the various foods you've become intolerant of. You've got to take your medicine faithfully and possibly use fungicide enemas. You may have to get rid of synthetic materials in your home and replace them with natural fabrics. It isn't fun!

Get all the help you can, because you're too tired to do everything yourself. If you can get a friend to do food shopping, help you fix meals in advance or clean up your apartment, accept their help. You need to rest as much as possible.

The only consolation I can offer is that candidiasis *is* curable. And most patients are relieved when they can identify it as a physical disease, not an emotional response. Month by month, your strength and spirit will come back. And someday, you'll be out there with the rest of us, overworking and overplaying, just like you always did!

25

What Have They Got That You Don't Have? Psychological Secrets of the Energy Superstars

Do you have enough energy?

Of course not.

I've never met anyone who'll admit to being energetic and productive enough.

When I phoned Henry Marsh, an Olympic athlete, to talk about his energy secrets, he said, "What makes you think I have a lot of energy?"

I wrote to Isaac Asimov, who's published over three hundred books, to see if he'd share his approach. He wrote back:

> Sorry, but I don't think you would want to interview me.
>
> Far from being high-energy, I'm the laziest man in the world.
>
> I do all my work sitting down. The only reason I keep writing all the time is that I am afraid that if I leave the typewriter even for an instant, someone will put me to work doing something that requires my standing or (worse yet) moving about.

Of course, he was joking; but the truth is, most people think they *should* have more energy. And when they say "should," you can hear the moral judgment in it: they're *guilty* of not having enough energy.

I don't know if this attitude is purely American, or if all people feel this way; but Americans certainly do. That guilty, never-enough feeling can be a real energy killer. It's certainly a fun killer.

One of the first psychological secrets I can give you for increasing your energy is:

1. *Lower your standards a tad.*

To put it some other ways:

- Don't expect so much of yourself.
- Give yourself some credit.
- Figure out how much is enough.

A patient once told me there must be something wrong with him because he didn't have the stamina to do all the things he should be doing—studying Italian before his trip to Europe, taking tennis lessons to improve his score and searching for country real estate—all this in addition to his job, social life and exercise schedule.

I told him to write down a hypothetical schedule of the week he'd like to live.

When he came back the next week, he had learned something. The only way he could do all his "shoulds" was by running from one appointment to the other, every day of the week. There wasn't a moment in any day without a job written in.

I didn't have to tell him that this is no way to live. At least, not for most of us. If you're truly comfortable living that way, that's fine.

But if you've always got a blur of undone tasks in the back of your mind—things you "should" be doing—try writing them into a one-week schedule. Then decide whether that's the kind of life you want.

The nagging of unfilled orders is very wearing. It makes you never satisfied with what you've accomplished. You never step back to look at the wall you've just painted and say, "Hey, that looks good!"

Decide what's most important to you and do it. That means you have to learn to live with undone tasks.

What if you suddenly realize you haven't done the laundry for three weeks? Congratulate yourself on that undone laundry. Congratulate yourself on all the things you haven't done; it means you've been doing something more important.

You'll get to the laundry eventually, or you'll find someone to do it for you.

Take naps. Dr. George Sheehan, the running guru, would never be accused of laziness. But he has times when, instead of taking a run a day, he takes a nap a day.

Haven't you started that yet? If you're a procrastinator, does that mean you're lazy? I doubt it. It may mean that you're a perfectionist. There's no way you can do the job as well as you think it should be done. So you're afraid to get started.

Remember, anything worth doing is worth doing badly. That's one of my favorite slogans for getting myself started on a job.

The first crack you take at a job *should* be off the mark. Why not? You're not doing the fine strokes, you're just roughing out a general idea. You'll make mistakes. But after the first few attempts, you won't be making the *same* mistakes.

Say you've got to learn a chapter in a book. The first time, just run through the chapter, seeing what information you can pick up. Don't focus on what you don't understand or can't remember. Just go for what's interesting. Next round, you'll pick up something else.

Each time you go back to work on a project, aim to make one or two improvements over the last time. That's all. You're never aiming for perfection; just a few small changes. And appreciate each improvement you make!

That's part of my next rule:

2. Pay more attention to what you're doing. Worry less about when it will be done.

Psychologists call this paying attention to the process, not the result. This method is very relaxing and it guarantees success. If you take care of walking each step, there's no question that you'll reach your destination.

You can even look at the scenery, talk to the natives, and sample the local cuisine as you go.

In terms of work, this means: If you have to make a business phone call, you can enjoy the person you're talking to, instead of just getting the job done. "Hey, how's the weather in Denver?" you ask. The person on the other end will tell you something interesting.

There *is* a time to think about when the job will get done. To think about it, not worry about it. Every now and then, see how much progress you've made and what your deadline is. If you won't be able to make the deadline, speak to the person who's expecting the finished job.

If the deadline can't be changed, you have some choices: Drop something else you're doing to focus on Priority One. Or arrange to do the job differently. Get the most important part finished by Deadline Day; schedule the rest for later. Or get someone else to do part.

It's important to evaluate your progress frequently, to be sure you can make your deadline. Otherwise, you'll worry about it instead of working with a clear mind. Once you've done this planning, forget about it. Put your mind on the job itself; don't worry about the goal.

Here's another way of saying "focus on taking each step, not on the end result":

3. Take it for granted that you'll achieve what you set out to do.

When a child is learning to walk, the parents *assume* he or she will soon be walking successfully. They don't say, "Well, maybe you don't have the talent for it," or "Maybe you should be satisfied with crawling: don't be so pushy."

No, the parents simply say, "Keep doing it and you'll surely get the idea. There's no doubt about it." They also add cheers and encouragement. Use this same matter-of-fact attitude toward every task. When you fall, notice why you fell. Then correct your technique.

All this is a lot easier said than done, especially if you've been taught that success is for some people but not for you. Too many of us get that message.

The five high-energy people you'll meet here were all taught that it's natural to succeed. John Sculley, CEO of Apple Computer, was taught that his efforts were worthwhile; that he could accomplish something. Walter Channing, who built a fortune in business and a career in the arts, was taught to believe in his own inclinations. It didn't matter if the world around him disagreed.

Even Francine Ward, who went in the wrong direction for many years, had some good success models. Her mother put herself through college and graduate school at night while raising two children on her own. Her grandmother worked as a seamstress and always told Francine she could accomplish what she wanted.

If you've been raised with a lot of "failure" messages, you'll have to reeducate yourself. One way is by associating with "can-do" people. Stay away from complainers. Stay away from people who believe the company owes them something.

Maybe the company *does* owe you something. Take action and get it. Don't waste time complaining about it.

Successful people know that they're the center of their universe. All action comes from you. If you wait for someone to realize that you deserve better, it will never happen. Take one step at a time, and get it for yourself.

I'm introducing you to five high-energy people to show you some successful attitudes. Tune in to them.

And tune in to the winners in your own life.

4. Get psychological help if you have tough barriers to energy.

A very realistic way to correct bad attitudes is to get professional help.

If you wanted to learn to play golf or the piano, you'd pay someone to show you how. You can learn new attitudes the same way: with an expert's help.

Where I live, in New York City, going to a therapist is very ordinary and accepted. It's like going to the ear doctor or to a night class in bookkeeping.

"Hey, I gotta get out of here, this is my therapy day," someone will say in the middle of a meeting. No one gives it a second thought.

I realize therapy is not so accepted in some cities and towns. Try to pick up a relaxed attitude about getting psychological help. It's no stranger than going to the dentist or any other doctor.

Don't imagine that a strong, self-sufficient person would do everything himself. That's just another perfectionistic attitude, and perfectionism is the enemy of success. Give yourself a break. Learn to ask for help and use it. Learn to enjoy life. When you do, energy comes naturally.

In the next chapters you'll meet some people who've developed the knack. See what you can learn from them.

26

John Sculley: CEO of Apple Computer
When Standing Still Is More Tiring Than Change

There's a place in twentieth-century America where most people work twelve hours a day with no overtime pay. There are virtually no labor unions and few low-skill workers.

If you have plans for the weekend, you drop them at a moment's notice for a job emergency.

Free time? Most people spend it talking about work.

Marriage and social life? You'd better choose someone in the same industry; a spouse who's not in the business couldn't put up with the long work hours and total absorption. There's a lot of divorce and remarrying in this town.

And job security simply isn't considered; the local industry is constantly rocked by competition. The rate of business failure is high.

This is Silicon Valley, former prune country near San Jose. Here, America's computer industry was born and is being reinvented every day. Some people say Silicon Valley is the energy center of the country.

The "ordinary" workers here were the geniuses and overachievers of their colleges and grad schools. They were the the bookworms, weenies, nerds. Now they're here—happy in Nerdland, where everyone is super smart and totally focused. Although people can make a lot of money, that's not why they work so hard. They simply love to work.

If that's what most folks are like in Silicon Valley, what kind of energy does it take to be a leader?

These were the thoughts that ran through my mind when I realized I had taken a seat next to John Sculley, CEO of Apple Computer, on an early morning flight to California.

I had first become aware of John Sculley in 1985, when the Adventures of Apple Computer were in the news almost every day. It was a real-life soap opera for computer fans; the press made the most of each cliff-hanging installment. Would the fiery young geniuses of Apple defeat the IBM Goliath? Or would they destroy themselves first?

Could John Sculley, a mature business type of 46, succeed in a Silicon Valley company where people over 30 not only weren't trusted, they didn't even exist?

And who was the good guy at Apple—the charismatic Steve Jobs, who dropped out of college to create the company? Or John Sculley, the miracle worker who'd engineered Pepsi's victory over Coke, and had been hired to transform Apple into a grown-up company?

As I settled myself and my briefcase into the plane that morning, I recalled this as a story I'd enjoyed following a few years ago. But now I couldn't help thinking how rough it must have been for all the players involved. I'd recently finished reading Sculley's own book about his transition from life in Corporate America to the trackless wilds of the silicon jungle.

A career change in midlife is never easy. It's something a lot of people are doing now, because our whole economy is shifting. If you're considering a change, you know how much hope and excitement you feel about the possibility. And how much fear and self-doubt. Are you foolish to consider leaving a twenty-year career for a dream? On the other hand, is it reckless to stay in place? Maybe the industry you're in now is changing so fast that your security will walk out the door before you do.

Perhaps you'll have to move yourself and your family to a different part of the country. You may have to learn a new and highly technical business. You may suddenly become the oldest person in the company. And the least experienced.

All these things happened to John Sculley. He had so much to learn about computers, he hired a tutor to walk around with him during his first month and tell him what was going on. It's got to be nerve-wracking to make decisions about a business you don't know much about—a business that's so new, it's still being invented.

Back in the plane, we eventually got airborne and the coffee-tea-or-milk cart was wheeled down the aisle. Sculley ordered a cup of hot water. It was about 7:00 A.M.

"You can wake up without caffeine?" I asked.

"I can now," he said.

Later he told me he used to drink as many as twenty Pepsis a day. Finally, he decided he had to get away from all the caffeine. If you've ever kicked a big caffeine habit, you know how tough it can be. For some people, it means headaches, tiredness and a temporary depression. This confirmed my feeling: Here's a person who knows when it's time for a change.

Later, when the food trays arrived, we both chose cereal and skim milk instead of sausages and eggs. Now it was easy to get onto one of my favorite subjects, which is how diet and exercise habits can affect your energy.

I knew that Sculley had been a regular morning runner since he was 30. When he was a bachelor living in Manhattan, he would get up at 4:30 in the morning and run in Central Park before taking the train out to Pepsi headquarters.

His diet then was Basic Fast Food—pizza and burgers. As we chatted, he told me that he still likes burgers and has them occasionally, but he usually has fish or chicken; he has to watch his cholesterol. If salmon is available, he orders that, since it's been reported as an effective cholesterol fighter.

For years, his favorite lunch has been peanut butter and jelly on white bread. He keeps the supplies in an office cabinet. Under his wife's influence, he now uses whole-wheat bread. And, when he doesn't have to stay on the phone through lunch, he walks over to the Apple cafeteria and puts together a salad at the salad bar. Then he sits and chats with the engineers as he eats.

His only supplement is a daily multivitamin.

Besides cutting out caffeine, Sculley has virtually cut out alcohol. He drinks mineral water and sometimes wine. Every now and then he'll eliminate the wine for a few months; he agrees with me that even a little alcohol can sap your energy.

So these changes in his eating habits—along with his lifetime running routine—have brought Sculley into the high-oxygen lifestyle.

It's still his custom to get up 4:30, take a 3- or 4-mile run, then come home to shower and skim five or six newspapers. He's at his desk by 7:30 A.M. and works till 5:30.

He takes about three weeks' vacation a year—very often at his home in Maine—and usually doesn't work weekends. But on weekends and on vacation, he can't resist getting on the computer, which is linked to his staff's computers, and sending out a few memos. Although he loves art and can sketch ideas during a discussion with the engineers, he doesn't draw or paint for his own pleasure. That's something he looks forward to in the future.

So, after five years, John Sculley is right at home in the high-powered life of the Valley.

It's quite a life. And sometimes, when you read about people who perform like this, you can feel overwhelmed. They seem almost superhuman. But I'll tell you one of their secrets: their lifestyle isn't too much for them because they're living exactly the way they want. To live any other way would be stressful.

The only time Sculley found it hard to get up in the morning was when he'd been president of Pepsi-Cola for a few years. His job was becoming repetitious. He was walking along a track he'd already covered a few times. If he'd stayed, he probably would have felt less and less energy.

His friends thought he was nuts to give up a job at the top and walk into all the uncertainty at Apple. Sculley had done the same kind of thing earlier in his career—made a "wrong" move because it was right for him.

When he was 30, he was zooming along the fast track; he was the youngest marketing director Pepsi-Cola had ever had. After he'd been doing the job for three years, he left it to take an assignment that had been career suicide to everyone before him. He agreed to run Pepsi Co's International Foods division.

This was an unassorted collection of badly run, money-losing companies scattered throughout Europe and Central and South America. Running them meant constant travel—crossing either the Atlantic or the Pacific Ocean every single week for two years—and dealing with a different set of regulations and bureaucracies in each country. No wonder this job had wrecked the careers of so many managers.

But it was right for John Sculley. There were no rules to follow; he had to make up solutions as he went along. It was a lot like the Apple situation he would step into ten years later.

For example, part of International Food was a potato chip company in Brazil. They desperately needed new machinery, but the government wouldn't allow them to import any. Even if it had been legal, the company wasn't making enough money to justify the expense of new machinery. So Sculley and his people scoured the U.S. for good used machinery. Then they they took it apart and smuggled the parts into Brazil in their suitcases.

This is the sort of life that keeps Sculley's spirit alive. Would it be right for everyone? Absolutely not. Just last night, while watching Johnny Carson, I saw a 97-year-old man who still gets up at dawn to run the tractor on his farm. He's totally clearheaded and sharp-witted. He has a beautiful 75-year-old ladyfriend in California and another woman back home in Illinois. This man has endless energy. He has spent his entire life in one place, doing one kind of work. That kind of existence would probably kill John Sculley.

So listening to your inner voice is a key to keeping your energy alive—if you can hear what it's saying. How come some people—like Sculley—do it fairly easily?

I think it's because he was always encouraged to follow his own path. Even as a child, his parents gave him the respect of believing he knew what was right for him.

When he was 11, they financed his interest in ham radio. When he was 14, he was working with electronic equipment to the extent that he was able to invent a color television tube. He actually designed a tube that worked; it was a truly impressive achievement. Did his father know that at the time? Maybe not; he didn't fully understand the technicalities. But he respected his son. He didn't pat John on the head and say, "That's nice; now go away, I'm busy." He helped his son find a patent attorney. He paid the considerable expense of having the invention patented. Unfortunately, someone beat Sculley to it by just a few weeks.

When it was time to choose a college, John wanted to study art; his father thought he should get a business background. They reached a compromise that let him do both.

Very few people get that kind of validation from their parents. But it certainly pays off. Twenty or thirty years later, it helps you make the right choices—to move on or stay where you are.

Sometimes, you don't need to change your job. You need to stay and change yourself.

Maybe you have to learn to assert yourself—to say what you want without anger and without fear. Until you learn that skill, you'll have problems, wherever you work.

Or maybe you've had a great deal of success in situations where you're the boss and other people are subordinates. Now you want to move up. The people you're dealing with now are smart and capable—they can't be ordered around. If you use your old method, you're going to fail.

People who believe in reincarnation talk about "karma." "I have to pay a karmic debt," or "I got rid of some old karma." They mean that they made a wrong choice in a former life. Now there's a lesson they must learn that relates to that old choice. If they don't learn it now, they'll be reborn and given another chance to learn.

Well, you don't have to believe in reincarnation to experience this sort of karma. If you don't fix your personality problems, they'll move with you no matter what job you take.

Deciding when and how to change can be tough. But change hurts most when you're fighting it.

Sooner or later, you'll give in. You'll take the first step on your new path. And then, you'll have all the energy you need.

27

Henry Marsh: Attorney and Olympic Runner
Getting Your License to Win

Some people are taught to lose.

"The meek shall inherit the earth."

"Good people are poor; the rich are proud and arrogant."

"Don't try to get ahead of others."

"What do you think—you're important?"

If you heard this kind of thing when you were too young to know better, chances are you didn't grow up to be president of a Fortune 500 company.

Brains, talent, and hard work don't make you a winner. Somewhere along the the line, you've got to be told it's all right to succeed. You need "permission to win."

Henry Marsh is an Olympic runner and an attorney. While he was going to law school, he was training full time and competing in world-class events. In 1980, he completed his second year of law school, was named the most outstanding male performer at the Olympic trials for track and field, and became father of a new baby boy (the first of four children).

In 1983, when fellow members of the U.S. World Championship team were competing in Stockholm, Henry was trying a case in Salt Lake City. He specialized in litigation—another kind of contest. He caught up with his team at a later race.

I've been following Henry Marsh's career for years—partly because I was a competitive runner myself in college, and also because I'd once met him at a race where he was competing and I was a spectator. Later, while working on this book, I got in touch with him again.

Henry said that if I was interested in high-energy people, I should speak to his mother; she was the real dynamo in the family! I did, and Virginia Marsh filled me in on how he'd grown up; what he was like as a kid. Through these conversations, I began to understand where he gets his amazing energy and persistence.

I had always been impressed with the fact that both of Henry's careers involved a lot of work. Lawyers work extremely long hours, and so do Olympic athletes. When I asked Henry to give me an idea of his schedule, he said that his hardest working days were probably during law school. "When you've got a job, you can more or less leave the work at the office. But in law school, it's a never-ending process."

At that time, a typical day started with a run of a few miles—"not a killer workout; that came later." His morning was spent in class. In the afternoon he took a break from school for his "real" training—two to three hours of running at a prescribed pace with prescribed rest periods. This was his intense workout of the day.

"You've got to be up for it, not just physically, but mentally. You gear yourself up to get through each run. Then you're still on a high when you finish. You gradually come off that and then about an hour later it hits you."

By the time the fatigue took over, he'd be home for dinner. After that he'd "try to recuperate." Recuperating meant sitting in front of an open book; but "nothing was sinking in. You glare at the page because you've sort of got a headache from your workout and you're just drained and it's hard to focus and concentrate." After about an hour, he'd start to feel awake again. Then he could continue studying all evening—either at home or back at school.

In spite of the punishing schedule, Henry says, "I found law intriguing—it was a real experience. If I hadn't been committed to running, I know I would have gotten more involved, gone out for *Law Review*. But you have to make choices."

After earning his degree, he joined a Salt Lake City firm. He made a deal with them: He would be paid by the hour and would not put in the sixteen-hour days usually expected of young associates. Once again, his schedule included a morning run before work, a two- or three-hour workout in the afternoon, and more legal work in the evening.

Like most people who accomplish a lot, Henry has incredible persistence. Qualifying for the Olympics seems like a tough enough goal. Henry has kept himself trained to an Olympic level for twelve years!

He qualified in 1980. That was the year America didn't go to the Olympics; he got an award from President Carter instead. In 1984, he qualified but came down with a virus just before the games. He competed and finished fourth, missing a medal by two-tenths of a second. As I'm writing this, he's eligible for the 1988 Trials; I'm betting he'll qualify again. There's only been one other American runner to qualify for four Olympic teams.

Where does a person get this kind of energy?

Very early in life, Henry Marsh was granted a full and total license to win.

He was born into a religion that not only tells people it's their obligation to succeed; it gives them steady training in accomplishing goals as they work on church and community projects. If you're a Mormon, worldly success is not opposed to goodness; they're all one package.

According to Mormon founder Joseph Smith, "a religion which has not the power to save people temporally and make them prosperous and happy here cannot be depended upon to save them spiritually." Children are raised on stories of how their forefathers succeeded in making the desert bloom; how persistence and unconquerable faith brought prosperity out of poverty and rejection.

At age 5, Henry attended a nursery school that taught the kids they should aim to be first. At everything.

"As kids, we didn't get a dollar for every A, like they do in some families," Henry told me. "It was just expected. You were complimented, but you weren't rewarded. I always got A in everything. So did the other seven kids."

Success and being in the public eye is an old custom in Henry's family. He was named for his maternal great grandfather, James Henry Moyle, one of the first Mormon attorneys. Moyle was also the first Mormon to hold high government office. He was Woodrow Wilson's assistant secretary of the treasury.

With this history, there was never the slightest doubt that it was OK to be a front runner.

While talking to Marsh about the source of his energy, I couldn't help thinking that this kind of family and religion would not work for everyone. Another person could be paralyzed by such high expectations; they could kill your energy.

Growing up Mormon may be like growing up in one of the new Asian-American families. Many of our young Vietnamese and Chinese Americans are performing amazing scholastic feats; they believe that to do less would be letting their families down. We read a lot about the successful ones among them—they're setting a new pace for everyone else in our universities. We hear less about the Asian kids who can't hit the top and feel guilty, depressed and anxious as a result.

So I'm not telling you to go for an A in everything, like Henry Marsh, or to work from morning till night. The best way of life for you may mean a few hours of exercise a week and sleeping late on Saturday. That's a healthy, energetic lifestyle, too.

What I want to point out is an attitude that might help you: knowing that it's OK to win.

Does that mean it's all right to beat other people, to get ahead of them? You bet. This is not what everyone is taught; some families really stress the virtue of humility and deprivation. It can be done very subtly; low achievers sometimes adopt an air of moral superiority toward successful people.

If that's the philosophy you were raised on, and you'd like to shake it, you might start by getting mad. You've been given a handicap, as much as if they'd put a brace on your leg to keep you from running. Changing that old belief can be your most important key to energy release.

Why not take a leaf from the Mormons' book?

For instance, here's one of Marsh's favorite Biblical quotations: "Know ye not that they which run in a race run all, but *one* receiveth the prize; so run that ye may obtain." There's permission to win, right from the Bible. The Scripture is very clearly saying:

Get ahead of other people—not by undercutting them, but by "running so as to win"—running properly.

For Henry, part of "running properly" means a lifetime of good health habits. He's been on the High-Oxygen Program all his life. The Mormon "Word of Wisdom" advises members to exercise regularly and follow a healthy diet. And for the past few years, Henry has even taken a pro-oxygenator, DMG. It was given to him by a trainer at Athletics West, the club that sponsors him.

Henry never had to break any bad habits—Mormons don't use alcohol or caffeine, and they don't smoke. They're counseled to eat moderately, including a monthly fast. Henry's mother always served "normal" American food—that is, not faddish and not vegetarian. She made whole-wheat bread and served plenty of fruits and vegetables. She says of all her kids, Henry seemed to like the natural-food approach, and he stayed with it.

He's not a vegetarian; he believes meat helps build him up when he's sick and his body's "broken down." But when he's feeling strong and running hard, he craves carbohydrates. He loves rice, pasta, potatoes. His eating schedule is unusual; he eats lightly all day. Then from dinner till bedtime, "I eat nonstop." That's because he runs twice a day, and you can't eat much just before or after running.

After his morning "warm-up" run, he has juice and toast. Before his long afternoon workout, a light lunch is all he can handle. So evening is the only time he can fit in the calories he needs.

He sleeps about seven hours a night. He doesn't take naps, even though he's wiped out after the afternoon workout. He just waits for the energy to come back.

This is a tough and strenuous life; it doesn't leave much time for smelling the roses. But it can be satisfying to know you're going for the best that's in you—even if it means training for the Olympics twelve years in a row. When you live that way, you know that, win or lose, you've given your all; you've run the course. It's not a bad way to go.

28

Carmen Jones: 72-Year-Old Entrepreneur
Her Fourth Career's the Best Yet!

"What about Winston Churchill? He drank brandy and smoked cigars every day of his life and he was active till he was 90."

People are always bringing up Winston Churchill and his cigars to prove that it's OK to ignore your health; it should take care of itself.

But for every Winston Churchill, there are thousands of Steve McQueens, people who live the macho fantasy of flaunting the rules—drinking, smoking, not eating properly—until they die in their forties. McQueen just made it to 50. Bob Fosse, the innovative choreographer and director, dramatized that attitude perfectly in his movie, *All That Jazz*. In the film, the hard-living Fosse-inspired director has a heart attack. He continues drinking and smoking in his hospital room; he's going to tough it out.

This kind of story is real life for many people. It seems we can get away with nutritional mistakes and "attitude" mistakes for a while. Then something happens.

It's not an accident that many people change their habits somewhere in midlife. You hit 30 or 35, and you realize those two packs a day are setting you up for a heart attack. So you get off the cigarettes; then you go on to make a lot more changes. Or you wake up at age 40 with a pot belly and aching back. So you lose weight and join a class at the Y for back exercises. You're on your way to a new lifestyle.

If no changes are made by the 45-to-50 period, many people find that the machinery starts breaking down.

Carmen Jones was always a dynamic, can-do woman. She "had it all"—family and career—before it was the fashion. She was always so involved in life, she says, "I never knew when I was tired."

I first spoke to Carmen a few years ago when I was in Illinois for a sports medicine convention. The newspaper had an item about a local pizza store that had been given an award by the American Heart Association. This intrigued me, so I took time out from my meetings to phone the store and ask to speak to the owner. I looked at the photo with the article—a happy, outgoing women in her sixties, the kind of pink-cheeked grandmother who's never been sick a day in her life. After we'd talked a while, I learned this wasn't exactly true.

Actually, Carmen Jones had a great start in life.

She was born on a farm. As far as she knew, it was normal to get up before sunrise to go out and care for the animals. She loved seeing the seasons change, watching the plants and animals grow. It was obvious that work and life are one: you grow food; you eat it. That makes you strong so you can enjoy life and go out and work some more.

Recreation was doing things with the family—talking and telling stories while you're sewing or putting up shelves in your bedroom; reading the Bible or making plans for improvements on the house and farm.

As she grew up, Carmen never learned any separation between working and living. The whole family might spend a few hours baking bread and pie—was that work or family fun? Going out early in the morning with your brothers and sisters to say good morning to the animals and give them their breakfast—was that labor, or just being with the people and animals you love? Painting the kitchen a bright new color before Easter—was that a chore or a refreshing creative outlet?

That's how Carmen grew up.

She married and had two children; as in most families, a second income was desirable, so she worked part time, selling household products for a direct-sales company. Later, she became distribution manager for her state. "I like working with people and I had excellent products, so I started earning good money. After a while I thought, why not open my own store?" Eventually, she did—a shop carrying cosmetics and a line of gift items.

By this time her first marriage had ended; her son and daughter were away at college. Carmen was still young and healthy—she was in her forties—and she was free to put all her time and energy into the business. Helping make her customers beautiful was fun; choosing the right gift items was challenging. She worked long hours, made all the decisions and paid all the bills—store rent, employee salaries, bills for merchandise and advertising. All this was stimulating—and stressful. It became easy to spend a bit more energy than she had.

Then came her second marriage, to Jess Jones. It changed her career as well as her name—her husband persuaded her to put her selling skill to work for him. She became marketing director of his wholesale food company.

In the sixties, frozen pizza was a new item, and Carmen's job was to sell the idea and the products to distributors—the middlemen who could place it in supermarkets.

Every week, she would get into her car and drive hundreds of miles, covering three states. At that time, there were virtually no women working in the wholesale food business in the Midwest. Carmen used this to her advantage. She loved wearing smart business clothes, including terrific hats. She would often show up at a buying office without an appointment and tell the secretary that Carmen Jones was here to see Mr. Distributor. The buyer would be curious and intrigued by the executive-looking woman in the reception room. Who was Carmen Jones? She would be sent in before the three or four salesmen who'd been waiting an hour.

Carmen knew how to get into an office, she knew how to sell, and she had a great product. The same flair with which she had promoted her cosmetics she now enlisted to sell Jess's frozen foods. J and N Pizza became the most successful frozen pizza in the Midwest.

But this job was even more stressful than her own business—in part because the wholesale food business was a man's world. She had to conquer biases and barriers that hadn't existed in her previous twenty years of selling. To make it worse, she was losing her vigor. Bit by bit over the years, her vibrant health had diminished. She had a variety of digestive problems and the never-quite-healthy feeling that goes with them. Her fingers and joints were getting stiffer—an arthritic condition that wasn't helped by the long hours of sitting in a car. She consulted doctors and kept working and the pain kept getting worse. When Jess wanted to retire, Carmen agreed.

In retirement, she moved around less. She fought the arthritis by quilting or crocheting—making things for her grandchildren. But, after an hour or two of sitting, she'd feel even stiffer. Eventually, walking a block was difficult and painful. She tried bed rest, but then it was even harder to get up. More and more foods disagreed with her. She had no energy or enthusiasm for life.

From being a busy, successful person, she became a near-invalid.

Now Carmen had a choice. She could give in to the pain and "old age" and sit her way through lonely, unproductive days. But she hadn't sat still in fifty years.

So she made some changes.

She finally found the medical help she needed—Dr. Richard Ariazi, a chiropractic physician who uses a wide variety of treatment methods. At first, she needed daily therapy and she could hardly walk; Jess could drive her to her appointments. But she started getting better right away.

So what had Carmen been doing wrong? Why did she get sick? Obviously, she never abused her health by using drugs or alcohol.

She simply worked a bit too hard with a bit too much stress. She made the common mistake of eating too much sugar, fat and protein and not enough raw foods and complex carbohydrates. These sound like minor sins, but the body can't live with them forever. Our physical machinery is very adaptive; it tries hard to get along on whatever we give it. But after a while, the strain of adapting takes its toll and our various mechanisms start breaking down.

For Carmen, one of the first steps was to start cleansing her body with raw vegetable juices. Eventually, this vitalized the liver, kidney, spleen and intestines. She still drinks raw vegetable juice every day.

Why did she need cleansing? How can a clean-living person, living in a nice, countrified town, get filled with toxins? I can't speak for Carmen's case, since I've never treated her; I didn't even know her when she was sick.

But, in general, we get loaded with toxins by eating foods that our bodies are not equipped to digest—too much fat and sugar; too many "refined," processed foods, instead of food that's raw or steamed or baked without additives. As the digestive system struggles to cope with unnatural substances, its supply of enzymes gets low. The digestive organs overwork. Eventually, they stop functioning at their best.

At this point—since the digestive system isn't working efficiently—you don't digest and eliminate all your food. These poorly metabolized materials become toxins (poisons). Your body stores them away in the liver, in fat tissues, in the lining of the arteries. As a result, your digestive system gets even worse; you're in a downward spiral. You feel "queasy" or "sensitive" when you eat. You're sluggish and tired and constipated.

When you start cleaning out the toxins, your energy improves. That's what happened to Carmen.

She got another energy boost when Dr. Ariazi gave her some pro-oxygenators: Siberian Ginseng, Korean Ginseng and DMG. She doesn't use the brand of DMG discussed earlier in this book; she gets it in a formulation that includes a number of other supplements.

Naturally, her diet changed drastically. She cut out sugar and refined carbohydrates. She started eating more fruit, vegetables and whole grains. She eats only a few ounces of chicken or fish a day, and no beef.

So Carmen is now on the High-Oxygen Diet. Even her pizza recipe fits these principles. She experimented until she created a delicious sauce with low salt and no sugar. For the sausage pizza, she doesn't use beef, because beef has fat marbled all through it.

Instead, she buys pork and has the fat trimmed off. This makes a leaner sausage that's very tasty. Her pizza is so healthful, it was given the award that first brought it to my attention.

Carmen was also advised to stop using pasteurized milk because the heat of pasteurization kills milk's enzymes. Dr. Ariazi feels that the lack of enzymes makes it harder for the body to utilize milk's calcium. If you want to use unpasteurized milk, make absolutely sure that the animal it comes from is disease-free. Since Carmen lives near a farming area, she was able to get raw goat's milk; she no longer uses cow's milk. (Some nutritionists believe that the protein in goat's milk is more suitable to human bodies and more easily utilized.)

Along with dietary changes, Carmen was given several physical therapies for the arthritis, as her doctor felt they were needed: acupuncture and acupressure; ultrasound and muscle-stimulating electric current; chiropractic adjustment and shiatsu massage. She still gets a variety of treatments; they keep her loosened up. Carmen still has some stiffness, but she keeps herself moving. Now she can live a happy and useful life, in spite of the pain.

As time passed and Carmen started feeling like her old self, she got bored. The quiet life of retirement didn't offer much to a person who had never taken it easy. "You can only spend so much time playing golf and visiting your grandchildren," she says.

She started thinking about the delicious pizza she had sold so successfully. Why not sell the same product in a different way— all prepared, but uncooked, ready to pop into your oven. Fresh pizza could only taste better than frozen. And baking up your own pizza at home was the sort of family activity she'd grown up with.

She tried to sell Jess on the idea of going back to work, but he wanted to stay retired. So once again, Carmen found a store to rent and went into business.

The new enterprise was a great adventure; her life was starting over. She threw herself into it and worked on every detail. One day, as Carmen and her hired crew of teenagers were setting up the store, a friend dropped by to kibitz. He joked that Carmen looked so happy, she had become a kid again. "Right!" she said. "This is the Kids Korner!"

That became the name of the business. It started to grow.

Then Jess had a stroke. He didn't recover well; he became virtually helpless and had to be moved into a nursing home. He died there in 1987.

Today, Carmen is 72. Kids Korner has over forty locations in eight states; it did $2½ million worth of business last year. She was nominated Illinois Business Person of the Year in 1985 and is a frequent guest on TV, including an appearance on NBC's *Today* show. She loves to tell people that she's been a cover girl several times and got her first centerfold when she was 71! (The *Chicago Tribune* did a two-page spread on the business.) She's enjoying her best career yet.

As Kids Korner grew, Carmen hired her daughter, Kathleen Gulko, to take care of the business end. Kathleen, a mother of four, has a degree in merchandising and had a successful career in retailing before she joined her mother's firm. She's responsible for the daily business, financial and administrative problems of an organization that's growing faster than anyone ever anticipated.

I was interested in hearing these two entrepreneurs talk about the energy required to create a million-dollar company. They both felt they were working better and more naturally now than they had in their previous careers—partly because they no longer have to fight the sexual bias that still exists in many businesses. Kathleen had chosen the fashion industry because she thought women would have more opportunity there; but she found there was sex discrimination, even in that field.

With that kind of struggle eliminated, they can now put all their energy into building the company. They make strategic decisions together; then Kathleen handles the executive end and Carmen works on "the people part." Besides her frequent media appearances, she spends a lot of time in the stores, keeping in touch with customers.

Carmen says she isn't working for money. She had plenty before she started. A big part of her pleasure is in helping young people, her franchisees, make money. Choosing the right people as franchisees is crucially important; she wants to make sure they have the qualities necessary to run a profitable store. She wants them to succeed.

Does she ever get tired? Sure. But now when she's tired, she knows it. Whenever she feels overworked, she steps out into the small garden behind her apartment to do a little weeding, fertilizing or transplanting. She's back where she started: taking part in the wonder of helping things grow. If this is work, it's fine with her.

29

Walter Channing: Venture Capitalist, Sculptor, Triathlete
Discovering the Fun-and-Profit Motive

When he was in high school, Walter Channing's idea of being grown up was that he wouldn't have to do homework.

Today, he helps run several medical businesses in which he's invested millions of his own and other people's dollars.

His views on homework haven't changed.

He never takes stacks of reading home at night.

On weekends, he's completely occupied creating sculptures in the country studio he shares with his two young daughters, growing grapes for his own brand of wine, and biking, running and swimming around Long Island, training for a triathlon.

Walter earns his money in a way most people would consider very stressful—investing in new companies. He specializes in the medical field. Sometimes the companies are so new, they're still just an idea in someone's mind, or a formula in a laboratory.

Funding a business that won't make a profit till five years from now, if ever, has to cause a bit of anxiety. Especially if you're persuading other people to take the plunge with you.

Walter and his two partners not only help finance the businesses; they also take an active part in running several companies. That can mean funding the research it takes to develop an invention, figuring out how to turn it into a practical business, then searching for the personnel to run it. Next, they find other investors to help pay the bills. They also oversee the critical first few weeks and continue to sit on the board to help with key decisions.

To me this looks like a lot of hard work, tough decisions and uncertainty.

Walter not only doesn't think his job is unusually stressful; he feels he's a fairly free spirit, working in exactly the way he wants. In the process, he and his partners have built their company, CW Group, into the country's largest venture capital fund in the medical field.

"I always knew I wanted to make dough and have a good time doing it," Walter told me. "And it's working out okay. Sometimes I'll have to read a term sheet in the evening, or make some phone calls after dinner. But generally, I work from 8:30 in the morning till 6:00 or 6:30 in the evening. Of course, when there are crises in a start-up company, I might be on the phone around the clock. But that's stimulating, it's not boring. Look, I want the luxury of making money, having a good time doing it, being intellectually stimulated by my work and working when I want to. That's asking a lot. But it's the only way I can do it. I couldn't work in a boring job. I'd go crazy."

So Walter's approach is entirely different from the yuppies and hard-driving tycoons we read so much about. You know the recommended lifestyle: work long hours, send out for dinner, eat and fall asleep.

Movies about big business make the tension and anxiety seem glamorous: close-ups of jaws clenching; the calculating eyes of business panthers seeking each other's weak spots; heart-thumping music in the background. It's very dramatic.

When you watch Walter, you get the feeling that he's working, but it isn't hard; he doesn't have to screw his determination to the task.

His office is near the window, not far up from the street, because he likes to watch what's going on outside. Remember your school days, when you'd gaze out the window and not hear what was going on? "Never *mind* what's going on out there," the teacher would snap. "The answer is *here*"—WHAP! the pointer hits the blackboard—"*not* out there!"

How great to be grown up! Now Walter says diversions and daydreams are an important part of how he gets things done. In the middle of an intense phone conversation, he'll become captivated by a scene outdoors, so he'll interrupt the business discussion to tell his caller all about it.

The author Tom Wolfe lives in the neighborhood; he's a friend of Walter's. When he walks by, Walter leans out the window to yell hello. The parade of attractive women provides a diversion, as do the garbage collectors and antique cars and wildly dressed people who roam the isle of Manhattan.

The street and all its happenings are part of Walter's office. Inside, there are no walls around his desk area. The different parts of his life move freely in and out. His wood sculptures—body shapes carved from curvaceous trees—look just right lounging around the clean, modern office furniture. Walter's daughters often come in after school, as do partner Barry Weinberg's.

Walter lets friends use desk space for their own projects. When film producer Stephanie McLuhan (Marshall McLuhan's daughter) is in town, she uses one of the desks as her production office.

People from a company he sold three years ago often invade the office with bottles of champagne and a birthday cake. Then everything stops for a celebration. In the middle of the festivities, Walter will take a phone call to settle a problem in one of his companies.

He works this way on all his projects—real estate, wine horticulture or preparing for the venture capital course he teaches at NYU. And his way is amazingly productive, in every part of his life. Although he can only work on sculpture on weekends, he's had several one-man shows. His work is purchased by collectors and museums. Managing his real estate—he owns 130 acres in Long Island's Hamptons—gets done somewhere between office work and weekend relaxing. His wine project is progressing; after testing several types of grapes, he finally has his first hundred gallons of Chardonnay in casks.

I wondered if there were any "schoolteachers" in Walter's life today. "Not really," he said. "Some of the partners in these deals get irritated with my work style when things are going wrong. What the hell, when there's a lot of money at stake and you're anxious, the work style is something to blame. But usually, they're not routine people either. They know that plodding isn't always the fastest way to get there. Some of my best solutions come when I'm running or swimming. Or an idea will jell while I'm working on a sculpture on Saturday afternoon. Then I can make a couple of phone calls and clear up a problem that's been bugging us for months."

As I got to know Walter, I kept wondering how he'd acquired his great attitude toward work and his continual flow of energy. I imagined he must have been a successful 8-year-old, a dynamic teenager and a top-ranking college student. I was wrong.

Walter says he was a "juvenile delinquent" all through his youth. He must have been a fairly benign young criminal, since he grew up in a respectable Boston family, graduated from a fine prep school and Harvard, and never got into trouble with the law. I guess juvenile delinquency is a relative condition.

But he did go through his early years feeling like a low achiever; he didn't measure up and he knew it. He got poor marks, sought recognition through rebellious behavior, didn't have the approval of his teachers, and never won the respect of his peers, either in the classroom or in sports. He said he daydreamed through school and didn't have teachers who would take the time to see if a daydreaming kid was worth working with.

When he absolutely had to have good marks to move on to high school or college, he frantically organized himself to get the grades he needed. Then he drifted back to low achievement.

But how did he move from that . . . right into a successful, high-powered career? And how did he get through Harvard Business School? I assume he couldn't fake it—it's known as a place where hard work is required. "Well, I guess it is," Walter said. "But business school is the shortest of all the graduate programs. You only have to do it for eighteen months."

Since he wasn't stupid, Walter's parents and teachers assumed he was lazy. There was a general understanding that he was at the very least a problem personality. And at worst, a darned ungrateful kid, since his parents made real sacrifices to send him to good schools.

I asked Walter how he had given himself a feeling of importance when he was young. "By being a vandal," he said. "I was always on the brink of being thrown out of school."

One of his early enterprises, in sixth grade, was selling switchblades and condoms to fellow students at three times his purchase price. He bought the knives by mail order, after reading ads in a *Field and Stream* he found in the school library. The condoms came from the local drugstore. Condoms were a valued status symbol around school. It was a risqué joke to use them as balloons; it was daring and debonair to carry one in your wallet. Walter had sales representatives in all the classrooms, "Avon" gentlemen who distributed his wares and earned a commission. The discovery of his network led to one of his many near-dismissals from school.

People who grow up the way Walter did—with disapproval from grown-ups and no respect from peers, using rebellion as a way of feeling important—often continue the negative attention-getting all their lives. Or they may become compulsively "better than." They try desperately to associate with celebrities; they have to be the richest or the chicest or any -est that will dull the feeling of worthlessness.

What's unusual is for a "juvenile delinquent" to move right into a business that demands true confidence in one's judgment, and to succeed in it for twenty years. And that's what the venture capital business demands. There's no way to predict, scientifically, which companies, out of the hundreds you examine, to put your money on. Which will go under in the first few years? Which will survive—but barely? And which will not only work, but will make an excellent profit, and maybe be snapped up by a bigger company, at a healthy price?

No matter how many facts you gather, the final decision demands intuition and gut judgment. In other words, faith in your own instincts. Faith in yourself.

This is the business Walter went into, in his twenties.

Even earlier than that, he had taken another kind of step into adulthood; like a lot of aggressive men, he married young. As soon as he got his undergraduate degree, he married a Radcliffe undergraduate, Susan Stockard. She became the actress, Stockard Channing. The marriage lasted a few years.

After graduate school came a few years of apprenticeship, working for someone else—then into his own business.

When I asked Walter how he had managed to keep faith in himself, through years of nonachievement and disapproval at school, he seemed puzzled by the question. "Well—what choice did I have?"

Later, I asked the same question a few different ways and got the same sort of answer. I got the impression that believing in himself came so naturally to Walter, he didn't know what I was talking about.

The physical source of his aggressiveness and productivity was very clear to me; over the years, he's adopted more and more of the High-Oxygen Program.

He wasn't much of an athlete in school, except for skiing. But he started doing a little running a few years ago, and eventually bought a treadmill for his apartment and a Nordic Track machine for the office. Then he discovered triathlons, and that became his way of doing a great deal of exercise in a way that he enjoys. He's not the sort of person who'll practice self-discipline, week in, week out. But the competitiveness and exaggerated achievement of a triathlon appeal to him.

So, a few times a year, he challenges his friends and business associates to a triathlon. Then he gets on a training schedule. Before a race, he runs 30 miles a week, bikes 100 miles and swims 6 miles. He takes four-day weekends to do the swimming and biking. The running is done in the city—either in the park or on the treadmill in his apartment. He never achieves record-setting times in a triathlon; but the training does a lot for his health. When he's not working toward a race, he does maintenance exercise—running or biking every other day; swimming on weekends.

He's also eased his way into high-oxygen eating. His kitchen, both at home and in the office, is stocked with skim milk and decaffeinated coffee. The conference rooms at CW Group used to have dishes of candy on the tables; now, there are bowls of fresh fruit. Gradually, he's cut out beef in favor of fish and chicken. At cocktail time, he usually drinks wine or mineral water instead of a hard liquor.

But sometimes, he'll plan a lavish business dinner at the Century Club—a fatty gourmet feast, complete with cocktails, hors d'oeuvres, two wines, meat with a rich sauce, cheese and a deliciously decadent French dessert.

He takes vitamins and other food supplements, including a pro-oxygenator, Ginsana.

So Walter's method is to be strict sometimes and self-indulgent sometimes. Although he's never measured his maximum oxygen intake, his energy level suggests it's high.

I know the physical source of Walter's energy; but the emotional/psychological part was always a mystery to me. I felt it was worth digging a little, because most people would love to learn his knack of accomplishing a lot while still feeling free.

I believe I found the answer in his family history. I discovered that the Channings have a two-hundred-year tradition of doing it their way and succeeding very nicely.

William Ellery Channing, who was valedictorian of the Harvard class of 1798, came close to boycotting his own graduation ceremony. He felt the college administration was restricting his freedom by putting limits on what he could say in his valedictory speech. His friends assured him they'd all respect him immensely if he refused his degree; but his parents persuaded him to accept the concessions the college was offering.

Later, as a minister, Channing was the leader of a dissident movement that became the Unitarian church—a center of religious liberalism and personal freedom. He also worked for the rights of labor and against slavery.

William Channing's younger brother, Walter, actually *was* denied his college degree; he was one of the leaders of Harvard's "Rebellion of 1808." But the disgrace was only temporary; he was given a degree a few years later and eventually became a physician and dean of the Harvard Medical College.

Another Channing, William Francis, got his degree in medicine, but decided he didn't want to practice; he'd rather invent things. He invented the first electric fire alarm system.

Yet another career-switcher was William Henry Channing. An ordained minister, he decided that the Gospels are unreliable as history and that Christianity is not a divine institution; so he resigned his pastorate in 1841. He went on to a happy career as leader of nonreligious seekers of human freedom. He fought for the emancipation of women and was part of the underground railroad that helped escaping slaves.

A second William Ellery Channing—nephew of the first one— spent only a few months at Harvard. He found the whole experience irrelevant, so he left. When his family caught up with him, he was sitting in a furnished room, writing poetry. Harvard was willing to try again, but Ellery wasn't interested. He went on to publish several volumes of poetry and religious criticism (he was a friend of Thoreau and Emerson). He also worked as a journalist; for a while, he wrote for Horace Greeley's *Tribune*.

So in the Channing family, the message seems to be: Go ahead and follow your own path. You can rebel. You can drop out of college, and even out of religion. You can change your career. And if no one agrees with you, that's perfectly all right.

I don't think Walter was consciously focusing on all his dissident ancestors as he struggled through school—daydreaming, manufacturing guns and bombs, getting caught smoking, being given "Final Warnings."

But somehow, a family carries a tradition and values; and somehow they communicate them. Part of his family's value system is: Following your inner voice is important. Education is important. Making something of yourself—whatever that means to you—is important. Being rich is not important.

Walter says he developed a money-making urge because he always went to school with rich kids. He was annoyed and frustrated when he couldn't do the things his friends were doing.

Since answering the question "Where do they get the energy?" is a longtime hobby of mine, I got great satisfaction out of solving this little mystery. I got a true shock when I read a quote from the first William Ellery Channing, the Unitarian founder. He wrote,

"I desire to escape the narrow walls of a particular church, and to live under the open sky, looking far and wide and seeing with my own eyes and hearing with my own ears." When I read this, I remembered something Walter had said to me when we were talking about movies. "I just don't go to movies," he said. "I can't stand spending two and a half hours seeing the world through someone else's perception. I'd rather be sitting on the curb, looking at a piece of dog crap on the street, because then I'm using my own perception." Reading his ancestor's words, I had the eerie feeling that these two Channings were the same person.

And I had to smile at a description of this same Channing's grandparents. According to his biographer, "his grandparents, upon the father's and the mother's side alike, were persons of more than common energy, both in character and intelligence."

So I think it's fair to say that, in the energy game, Walter was given a very good start.

We can't go back and choose our ancestors. But maybe we can learn to work more by following our own bent and less because we've got to pay the bills. People who follow their inner direction usually do an excellent job of paying the bills.

We can allow work to be more fun. If you can work with the television on, do it. Stop thinking you have to give a hundred percent concentration, a hundred percent of the time. Interrupt a business session to share a funny or bizarre thought with your coworker. When you can't concentrate on the list of numbers in front of you because you start thinking of a fun plan for the weekend—take ten minutes to phone a friend and get the plan started. Then you'll have a good reason to zip through your work faster.

If you find that you're an oddball and an underachiever in your company, maybe you're in the wrong place. Why work with people who can't use what you've got to offer? When your mind wanders from your work, pay attention to where it goes. Maybe you can go with it. You may find a lot more fun and money there.

30

Francine Ward: From Bronx Ghetto to Georgetown Law
Dreaming—It's the First Step in Doing

Daydreams can be dangerous. You can use them to escape life.

You can also use them to build a new one.

Suppose you were 28 years old before you faced the fact that your dreams had led to a dead end. All your life, you've done nothing but "pretty girl" jobs—you've been paid to smile. Now even your looks are running out; you've turned into an old and tired 28. You never exercise, you smoke three packs of cigarettes a day, you live on steak and champagne, and you're 30 pounds overweight.

Being a pretty, charming black woman got you out of the South Bronx, but it hasn't gotten you to where you want to be. You've never had an office job because you can't type. In fact, you never got your high school diploma.

Now what?

At age 28, you get the idea that you'd like to be a lawyer.

Lotsa luck!

That's how many people reacted, seven years ago, when Francine Ward decided to change her life. They didn't hesitate to tell her how slim her chances were.

Today, at 35, Francine is more than halfway through Georgetown Law School. She's on *Law Review,* an honor reserved for the most qualified students. This summer, she'll be working as an attorney; her job as summer associate at a leading New York firm carries such a high salary, she's embarrassed to let me quote it. She says she still can't type; she hunts and pecks on her home computer as she organizes her study notes and writes articles for the law journal.

Francine's story would be inspiring to anyone, but it should be especially interesting to women. Her life is almost a capsulization of the change in women's consciousness.

As soon as she learned to read, Francine used books for escape. She had a lot to escape from: a poverty that was so real she remembers picking bits of plaster off the walls and sucking on them to quiet her hunger. Her overall feeling was hunger and emptiness. She felt ignored and put aside for her sister, who's thirteen months younger.

Her mother, a librarian, often talked about the children she worked with during the day. Francine felt there was love for every child but herself; she resented her mother, her sister and all the kids in the library. She met her father just once, after she was grown. There was an uncle who loved her, but he got married and moved to Chicago; that gave Francine another woman to hate. She developed a full-blown case of the old-fashioned female attitude: other women were rivals and enemies.

But her mother filled their apartment with books, and Francine used them to kill the pain. From age 6 to 14, the world of books was more real to her than the streets of the South Bronx.

I heard Francine's life story, bit by bit, during long runs in Central Park. New York is supposed to be a big, impersonal town. Actually, it's hundreds of little villages—groups of people who come together through mutual interest. We become as friendly and gossipy as people in a small town. Runners are one of these communities. If you run regularly in one place—the park, for instance—you get to know each other's lives and hopes and work problems.

I had to laugh when Francine told me that her early role model was Madame Bovary. Emma Bovary, a nineteenth-century airhead who escaped her boring marriage by burying herself in popular romantic novels—she was the equivalent of a modern housewife who's more involved in the soaps than in her own life. Emma's dreamworld led her to adultery and debt and suicide. Francine's imagination started her along a similar path.

In high school, her escape was activity and sociability. "I was always on some committee; in my senior year, I was treasurer of the student government. Everyone knew me, yet I always felt like an outsider. My life was a continuous effort to be 'on,' to look like the vivacious, outgoing girl. That's a frightening way to live when you believe you're a fraud."

She went to the High School of Art and Design and majored in photography—a good choice for such a visual person. This high school is on East 57th Street, in one of the best neighborhoods in Manhattan. There Francine saw women who looked different from the ones in her own neighborhood. She saw them coming out of apartment buildings that had awnings and uniformed doormen. As she walked to school from the subway every morning, she started focusing on a particular building on East 58th Street. She kept thinking, "I'm going to live there some day." Years later, she did.

She never bothered to get her high school diploma because it would have meant going to summer school to make up a course she had failed. On the day her classmates were posing for pictures in caps and gowns, she was out buying eight different styles of sunglasses, trying to get a pair that would please her new boss, a fashion photographer.

Now her life was shaping up—she was living her dreams! At least, part time. Through her job, she met men who were happy to introduce her to the Manhattan of the 1970s, a world of private clubs and celebrity discos that a young photographer's assistant could never afford on her own.

In the evening, she lived her fantasies. She spent every penny on the clothes she needed to fit in. During the day, she was an underpaid assistant, catering to a temperamental boss, demanding clients and beautiful models. It seemed easier to live in her imagination than to pay the dues it takes to succeed in the competitive world of commercial photography. More often than not, she sleepwalked through the day, fighting off a hangover. The years clicked by and she was still a glorified gofer who knew a lot about lenses and f-stops. Her career was going nowhere.

But that was okay. Soon she saw another route to success.

New York State was going to legalize gambling. She would go to Las Vegas and learn how to be a croupier in gambling casinos. "My plan was, I'd come back home and be the first woman pit boss in New York." She saw herself wearing chic clothes and jewelry, presiding over a roomful of elegant people who dropped thousands of dollars a night. Now, *that* would be glamour! Francine never aimed low.

So she went to Las Vegas, seeking her pot of gold. It was like stepping into the darkness. She worked all night in smoke-filled rooms and seldom saw daylight. "Vegas was so decadent—all alcohol, drugs, money and sex. Everything was for sale."

Her job involved being charming to people whose moods were contingent on the roll of the dice. "Gamblers are strange; they feel the world owes them something and they're out to get it. They're superstitious. They think the dealer has the power to make them win."

So she smiled and remembered people's names and earned big tips. But she hated her life.

Then New York voted against legalized gambling. Another dream crashed. She was stuck in Vegas.

Crossing the street one night, she was hit by a car and broke her leg.

Now she was in total misery—angry, bitter and unemployed. She couldn't work for over nine months because she couldn't stand at the tables all night. She describes her overweight body as being filled with sugar, salt, fats and alcohol. Quite a difference from the lean, muscular woman I now saw running around the park at six every morning! In her Las Vegas days, Francine was hardly willing to walk to the corner.

Finally, one hot, dull Sunday, she hobbled into a church—a place she hadn't visited since she was 14. She happened to pick a Unity church. This faith teaches people to use their imagination to achieve their dreams. At services, they specifically guide the congregation in visualizing their goals, seeing themselves in the life they desire.

Changes started happening immediately—she felt the hint of a feeling of freedom. Her leg healed slowly and her spirit was healing too. Away from the casinos, she started meeting a new kind of person. One of the most important was Louise, a dynamic and successful woman in her late fifties. She became the primary guide on Francine's new road.

"Louise didn't baby me; she was enough of a friend to tell me that I was responsible for ruining my life. She challenged me to do something about it." But it took nearly two years to start getting through the sadness and anger and hurt pride. She was still smoking, still overweight, still hating her job at the casino.

Through Louise, Francine met other strong women—like June, who was going to law school. That caught her imagination right away. But she shrugged it off. June was only 21; Francine was pushing 30 and she hadn't even graduated from high school. It was too late for her. Nonetheless, she started studying for an equivalency diploma—secretly. "I had too much ego to let anyone know I didn't have a diploma. I was ashamed to sit in a classroom with young kids who were probably smarter than I. I got one of those Barron's GED books and studied it. When friends came over, I hid the book under the bed." The next time the test for the General Education Diploma came up, Francine took it and passed. She still didn't tell anyone.

Then she met Lynn. At 30, Lynn was attending the University of Nevada, studying business administration. Francine still couldn't see it for herself, until Lynn invited her to sit in on some classes. She absorbed the sights and sounds of the university, watching people of all ages attend school. Some went full time, some went in whatever hours they had free. Now her imagination had something to work with.

The next term, she enrolled.

Although it was hard to believe she could ever complete the journey, she always had a clear vision of where she wanted to be. She saw a room filled with law books—her own little den at home.

It had a highly polished wooden desk. The lighting was subdued and cozy. There was a phone she could pick up at any time of night to consult with colleagues.

From then on, "I just put one foot in front of the other." She started eating differently. One by one, she cut out caffeine, alcohol, red meat and sugar. She started eating raw fruits and vegetables. As the weight came off, she got interested in exercising.

Two weeks before her thirtieth birthday, she smoked her last cigarette.

She moved back to New York and enrolled at Hunter, a city college. There was no glamourous "pit boss" position to come back to. She couldn't even get a secretarial job, since she couldn't type. Instead, she worked as a plumber's assistant. "I helped build the Javits Convention Center."

Next came a job closer to her goal—as a paralegal in a small law firm. Her day would start at 5:00 A.M. because she wanted to be at the Vertical Club by 6:00 for a workout and run. Next, an 8:00 class; work at the law firm from 9:30 to 5:30; then more classes until 10:15.

I was interested to hear that she chose the Vertical Club—one of the most expensive in New York—when a low-priced club has basically the same equipment. But Francine always surrounds herself with the imagery of success and achievement.

Carrying sixteen credits at night, she completed her undergraduate degree in five years and was accepted at several law schools. Her choice was Georgetown University Law Center.

Today, living in Washington, her diet and lifestyle are just about perfect, although I think she should eat more frequently. She doesn't think of her routine as a "High-Oxygen Program" but that's exactly what it is. She gets up at six and has a protein drink and vitamins— she likes the Shaklee products. Next, a 4½-mile run before she goes to law school or to her job at the Securities and Exchange Commission. She works there two days a week.

Her next meal is around 3:00 P.M.; usually, she stops at a salad bar and picks up a big assortment of vegetables and protein— chicken or fish. If she's hungry in the evening, she eats fruit.

"My weakness is pasta and rice. When I'm very stressed and anxious, at exam time, I'll sometimes binge on pasta."

Her vitamins: a multivitamin; B complex, A and C; E plus selenium; calcium and magnesium; lecithin, iron, bee pollen and garlic. She says she tried ginseng but found it too stimulating. (She may have tried a brand that was spiked with caffeine; pure ginseng is not overstimulating.)

She gets to bed about midnight. "Sleeping late" on Saturday means getting up at 7:00 A.M. Her schedule leaves room for friends— new friends from work and school; old friends from New York who phone when they're in town. One of these friends is her mother. The two women have learned to see the very different lives they led in that same apartment long ago. "Getting to know my mother has been a wonderful gift."

The only thing missing is a relationship with a man, "which I know is a full-time job. I don't have the time for it now."

Francine says her energy comes from her faith. She knows God will give her the strength to keep putting one foot in front of the other. With the power of her imagination, she's been able to transform the "fire-and-brimstone" God of her childhood into a completely different being. Her Southern Baptist God was an old man sitting on high, judging. Her new God was, for a while, female. Now it's usually a neutral entity. But it's always something that wants her to win. "I guess I'm in a partnership with God. That's probably the best way to put it." Getting her new God did not come easily, either. She had to work at it, work to get rid of the old punishing images. "Everything is work," Francine says. "I've just stopped trying to get around it."

So if you've got a lively imagination, you've got a powerful weapon. It can send you into the misery of helpless escapism. Or it can keep you putting one foot in front of the other until your dreams become real.

31

Feeling Good and Making Good

Now what? Now that you've got a wealth of power at your fingertips—will you take it?

That's what I kept wondering, as I was writing this book.

You've learned the most effective energy-building techniques, from ancient practices to those based on the most advanced scientific thinking.

You've met exciting people who make the most of their power. They're building companies, breaking records, changing their lives. Just reading stuff like this makes you feel good.

I hope it doesn't make you feel too good.

The problem with so many "help" books is, you feel exhilarated just reading them. A few months later, you need another boost so you go on to the next book. And nothing has changed.

I've tried to make this a practical, hard-core-reality book, not a "feel-good-through-wishful-thinking" book.

I hope that, after reading it, you don't feel fulfilled and rewarded. I'd like you to feel a bit uncomfortable and dissatisfied. The fact is, it's very easy to get by in this country without trying too hard. In the first few years out of high school, most people are earning, not just the basics, but the clothes and cars and VCRs, without spectacular effort. And we see so much superluxury around us, it's easy to believe we're entitled. We're entitled to everything we want simply because we were born.

This country also gives us abundant opportunities for living in fantasy. New movies, old films on tape, escape through books or gossip or MTV—these are only the most harmless ways of avoiding life.

But for feeling good, nothing beats the feeling of really doing it; going for what you want and getting it.

So I'd love to know what you do with this new knowledge you have. I'm interested in hearing your experiences: which methods you use first, which are most effective, and how you use your new energy.

If you want to share your experience, please write me:

Daniel Hamner, M.D.
Peak Energy Press
3 East 68th Street
New York, NY 10021

Good luck!

32

A Week of Great Eating

1,500 calories per day:
Less than 30 percent fat;
15 percent protein, 55 percent carbohydrates

Some guidelines:

Calories. 1,500 calories is a reducing diet. For maintenance, a man weighing 150 pounds needs about 2,200 calories a day. A woman weighing 125 pounds needs about 1,800 calories.

Margarine. Choose a margarine that lists liquid safflower oil, liquid corn oil or liquid sunflower oil as the first ingredient on the label. Soft, tub margarines are better than stick margarines because they have a higher percentage of polyunsaturated fat.

"Free" vegetables are very low in calories and may be eaten in any amount: broccoli, Brussels sprouts, cabbage, lettuce (dark green, such as romaine or Boston), chicory, Chinese cabbage, endive, escarole, parsley, radishes.

Salad dressing. If you use regular salad dressing, limit the amount to 1 or 2 tablespoons per salad—depending on how much other fat you're having that day. If you use diet low-fat salad dressing, you can have up to 4 tablespoons.

Water. Drink eight to ten glasses a day.

Beverages. Coffee or tea should be limited to two cups per day. Instead of soft drinks, try plain water or seltzer with a squeeze of fresh lemon. It's refreshing, and has none of the artificial ingredients you get in most soft drinks.

Dilute orange juice with water or seltzer. Orange juice is very sweet and delivers a lot of sugar to your system in a very short time.

FIRST DAY

BREAKFAST:

Half grapefruit

½ cup shredded wheat or oatmeal

1 cup skim milk

Coffee or tea

LUNCH:

3 ounces skinless chicken, broiled

1 cup whole-grain rice

2 broccoli spears sprinkled with 1 teaspoon Parmesan cheese

Salad: unlimited (made with free vegetables and maximum 2 tablespoons low-fat dressing)

2 sesame breadsticks

DESSERT OR AFTERNOON SNACK:

1 cup low-fat cottage cheese with 2 fresh pineapple rings

DINNER:

Meatless soup, equal to 100 calories;
e.g., 1 cup barley soup or ¾ cup lentil soup

Carrot sticks and green pepper
(½ carrot and ½ green pepper)

1 cup strawberries

NIGHT SNACK:

½ cup plain low-fat yogurt with 1 ounce cereal (e.g., Nutri-Grain or other nonsugared cereal)

SECOND DAY

BREAKFAST:

¼ cup fresh blueberries

1-egg omelette (vegetable cooking spray or 2 teaspoons margarine to coat pan)

1 slice whole-grain bread with 1 teaspoon margarine

1 cup skim milk

Coffee or tea

LUNCH:

½ cup tomato juice

1 slice lean roast beef (3 ounces)

1 small baked or boiled potato, or ½ cup green peas

Salad: unlimited (made with free vegetables and maximum 2 tablespoons low-fat dressing or 1 tablespoon regular dressing)

1 small whole-grain roll with 2 teaspoons margarine

¼ cantaloupe (save for afternoon snack, if you like)

DINNER:

Soup, equal to 150 calories, made with 1 ounce lean meat or fish; e.g., 1 cup chicken/rice or 1 cup Manhattan clam chowder

6 small crackers (unsalted) with 2 teaspoons margarine

1 tomato, sliced

¾ cup low-fat yogurt with ½ banana

THIRD DAY

BREAKFAST:

½ cup grapefruit juice

2 ounces low-fat cheese (farmer or hoop cheese)

1½ slices whole-wheat toast with 1 teaspoon margarine

1 cup skim milk

Coffee or tea

LUNCH:

Baked fish: 4-ounce fillet stuffed with celery, onions and mushrooms

Baked potato topped with 1 tablespoon low-fat cheese

1 cup steamed carrots

1 slice whole-grain bread with 1 teaspoon margarine

1 orange (save for afternoon snack, if you like)

DINNER:

1½ cups ratatouille or vegetable soup made with 1½ ounces meat

2 slices whole-grain bread with 1 teaspoon margarine

1 medium baked apple

FOURTH DAY

BREAKFAST:

¾ cup oatmeal cooked with ¼ cup raisins

Coffee or tea

½ cup skim milk

LUNCH:

Broiled hamburger made with ¼ pound lean beef

2 slices onion

2 slices rye or whole-grain bread

1 peach or pear, in season

1 cup skim milk

(Or save fruit and milk for afternoon snack. Equivalent: ¼ cup frozen yogurt)

DINNER:

1 cup pasta with 4 tablespoons unsweetened tomato sauce

Top with steamed vegetables; e.g., broccoli and cauliflower

½ cup low-fat cottage cheese with 1 piece of fruit

FIFTH DAY

BREAKFAST:

1 orange

1 ½ ounces lean ham

1 bran muffin with 2 teaspoons margarine

1 cup skim milk

Coffee or tea

LUNCH:

3½ ounces broiled fish or skinless chicken

½ cup steamed or raw cauliflower

1 stalk asparagus, sprinkled with 1 teaspoon Parmesan cheese

½ cup whole-grain rice

1 slice French bread with 1 teaspoon margarine

1 piece of fruit (save for afternoon snack, if you wish)

DINNER:

1 cup New England clam chowder

Salad: unlimited (made with free vegetables and maximum 2 tablespoons low-fat dressing)

1 whole-grain roll or bagel with 2 teaspoons margarine

1 peach

SIXTH DAY

BREAKFAST:

½ cup orange juice, diluted with water or seltzer

½ cup cereal (may be with fruit, but not sugar)

Coffee or tea

1 cup plain low-fat yogurt or 1 cup skim milk (save for afternoon snack, if you wish)

LUNCH:

4 ounces broiled skinless breast of chicken

½ cup green beans with 1½ teaspoons margarine

¾ cup whole-grain rice

1 whole-grain hard roll

¾ cup strawberries, or other fruit (save for afternoon snack, if you wish)

1 cup skim milk (save for afternoon snack, if you wish)

DINNER:

1 cup pasta, with 2 teaspoons olive oil and 2 ounces fresh seafood (about 4 clams or 4 scallops or 4 mussels)

Salad: unlimited (made with free vegetables and maximum 2 tablespoons low-fat dressing)

Slice of melon

SEVENTH DAY

BREAKFAST:

Banana and orange slices (½ banana, 1 orange)

1 slice whole-grain toast with 1 teaspoon margarine

1 egg, boiled or poached

1 cup skim milk

Coffee or tea

LUNCH:

Broiled meat or fish kabob made with 3 ounces lean fish or meat, ½ cup onions, ½ green pepper, 1 teaspoon olive oil

Salad: unlimited (made with free vegetables and maximum 2 tablespoons low-fat dressing)

1 small whole-grain roll with 1½ teaspoons margarine

¼ cantaloupe (save for afternoon snack, if you wish)

DINNER:

¾ cup cooked beans and 2 ounces cooked, shredded lean beef or pork heated with 4 tablespoons unsweetened tomato sauce

2 tortillas

Salad: 1 cup spinach or unlimited free vegetables

1 cup skim milk

1 apple

Appendix:

Other Energy-Boosting Substances You May Have Heard About

Octacosonol and Wheat Germ Oil

Octacosonol is a factor found in wheat germ oil and other plant substances. Chemically, it's an octacosyl alcohol. Most of the testing on octacosonol and wheat germ oil was done by Thomas Kirk Cureton, Ph.D.; reports on forty-two of these experiments were published in 1972. Three of the experiments reported by Dr. Cureton measured VO_2 MAX and net oxygen debt. None of the three experiments gave irrefutably favorable results. Since octacosonol and wheat germ oil are not proven pro-oxygenators, I don't use them in my program.

However, the lack of results (in terms of oxygen boosting) may be a matter of inefficient testing methods and Dr. Cureton's own lack of interest in measuring VO_2 MAX. So these two substances *may* be pro-oxygenators; we simply don't have the tests to prove it.

Many of Dr. Cureton's tests do indicate the power of octacosonol and wheat germ oil to increase stamina.

His tests are published in *The Physiological Effect of Wheat Germ Oil on Humans in Exercise,* by Thomas Kirk Cureton, Ph.D. Publisher: Charles C. Thomas, Springfield, Illinois.

Coenzyme Q_{10}

Coenzyme Q_{10} is part of the electron transport system, which is located in the mitochondria (the cell's energy generators). This system is the final end product of both aerobic and anaerobic metabolism.

Most of the studies done on this substance are reported in *The Miracle Nutrient Coenzyme Q_{10}*, by Emile G. Bliznakov, M.D., and Gerald L. Hunt, published by Bantam Books in 1987.

The studies indicate that, when taken as a supplement, it increases the energy of individual cells and therefore improves the functioning of the organs formed by the cells. For instance, by energizing the cells of the heart, coenzyme Q_{10} apparently strengthens the heart.

Since coenzyme Q_{10} seems to improve cellular energy, it's reasonable to assume it would increase overall energy. However, I've only seen one study that tests its influence on stamina or speed or maximum oxygen intake. This study indicates that Q_{10} can increase oxygen usage somewhat in healthy sedentary men. See "Coenzyme Q_{10} and Physical Performance" by J. H. P. Vanfraechem in *Biomedical and Clinical Aspects of CoQ$_{10}$*, Vol. 5, edited by Folkers and Admura and published by Elsevier Science Publishing Co. in 1986.

I haven't reached the conclusion that CoQ_{10} is *not* an energy booster or a pro-oxygenator; it simply hasn't been sufficiently tested yet.

L-carnitine

L-carnitine is an amino acid that's involved in the process of turning fat into energy. It carries fatty acids across the cell's mitochondrial membrane.

Researchers who are interested in athletic performance have been exploring its possibilities; increasing fatty-acid breakdown in the body would be an endurance athlete's dream. If the body can make energy from fat, the glucose is saved for the end of the race.

But there have been no definitive studies as yet to prove or disprove L-carnitine's ability to aid the body in sparing glycogen.

One study showed that when L-carnitine was used by very active athletes, they lost weight and reduced their percentage of body fat. Some athletes are using it because of its role in fat burning; but don't take it in large doses without a physician's supervision.

So far, this substance has not proven to be a highly efficient pro-oxygenator. A study conducted at the University of Milan showed that taking L-carnitine for two weeks increased athletes' VO$_2$ MAX slightly (6 percent). So it's probably an energy booster; but not as effective as the two pro-oxygenators recommended in this book. In this same study, L-carnitine did not increase the users' ability to utilize fat (instead of stored glycogen) for energy.

There are several studies that indicate L-carnitine is extremely beneficial to people who are deficient in it; but it's not likely that most people have a deficiency. The body synthesizes a lot of its own L-carnitine, and it's available in food, especially meat.

Some Brand-Name "Energy Boosters"

As you go through your health food store, you'll find many products that claim to increase energy. If you read the labels, you'll find that some of them contain ginseng or octacosonol or even caffeine. Some simply specify "herbs." I suggest you write the company, asking for information, preferably test results, to document the claim of energy enhancement. Here are a few of the products you may find, with information I received from the distributors of the products.

Alive Energy—Auro Trading Co., 18A Hangar Way, Watsonville, CA 95076.
No information on ingredients or studies. Literature included advice on "visualizing health."

PAK—Enzymatic Therapy, Inc., Green Bay, WI 54305.
Literature includes some test results that indicate an increase in VO$_2$ MAX and a decrease in lactic acid. These tests suggest that this may be an effective product. I'm not including it in my program

at this point because it has not been tested as extensively as some other products.

Siberian Ginseng—Sun Chlorella Co., Ltd., 35 Bond Street, Westbury, NY 11590.
Information on Siberian Ginseng, which is one of the pro-oxygenators recommended in this book.

Natrol Guarana and Natrol High—Natrol, Inc., Chatsworth, CA 91311.
According to the information supplied by the company, the plant guarana is a source of caffeine; it has two and a half times more caffeine than coffee.

The second product, Natrol High, contains herbs, including ginseng and ma-huang. I'm not familiar with this second herb. According to an article in *Bestway's* magazine, it is nonaddictive and nontoxin and gives some people a "pleasantly energized feeling." The same article suggests that ma-huang affects the adrenaline response and diverts oxygen and energy to the surface of the body. For an excerciser, this is not beneficial; you want your blood and oxygen to go to the muscles. The article points out that internal organs, such as the digestive organs, would be depleted by this diversion of energy.

These distributors did not reply to a request for information:
Biotec Foods, 931 University Avenue, Suite 206, Honolulu, HI 968267.

Zoom—SNJ Enterprises, New York, NY 10003.

HMS Pep Products, Inc., 886 West Castleton Road, Box 715, Castle Rock, CO 80104.

Bibliography

Cholesterol, Pectin, EPA, Niacin

Baig, Mirza Mansoor, Ph.D., et al. "Pectin: Its Interaction with Serum Lipoproteins." *American Journal of Clinical Nutrition* 34 (1981): 50–53.

Burros, Marian. "Eating Well." *New York Times,* November 18, 1987.

Gsell, Daniela, M.D., et al. "Low Blood Cholesterol Associated with High-Calorie, High Saturated Fat Intakes in a Swiss Alpine Village Population." *American Journal of Clinical Nutrition* 10 (June 1962): 471.

Kanter, Yoram, et al. "Improved Glucose Tolerance and Insulin Response in Obese and Diabetic Patients on a Fiber-Enriched Diet." *Israeli Journal of Medical Science* 16 (1980): 1–6.

Kay, Ruth M., Ph.D., et al. "Effect of Citrus Pectin on Blood Lipids and Fecal Steroid Excretion in Man." *American Journal of Clinical Nutrition* 30 (February 1977): 171–75.

Taton, J. "Therapeutic Effects of Pectin Fortified Diet in Diabetes Mellitus Type 2." *Diabetologica* 21 (1981): 335.

Diet

Bicher, H. I., et al. "Effect of Microcirculation Changes on Brain Tissue Oxygenation." *American Journal of Physiology* 217 (1971): 689–707.

Cullen, Chester, et al. "Intravascular Aggregation and Adhesiveness of the Blood Elements Associated with Alimentary Lipemia and Injections of Large Molecular Substances." *Circulation* 9 (March 1954): 335.

Cummins, E. J. "Environmentally-induced changes in the brains of elderly rats." *Nature* 243 (1973): 516–18.

Denton, Derek. *The Hunger for Salt.* Berlin: Springer-Verlag, 1982.

Dustman, Robert E., Ph.D., et al. "Aerobic Exercise Training and Improved Neuropsychological Function of Older Individuals." *Neurobiology of Aging* 5 (1984): 35–42.

Edwards, Miles J., et al. "Improved Oxygen Release: an Adaptation of

Mature Red Cells to Hypoxia." *Journal of Clinical Investigation* 47 (1968): 1851.

Friedman, Myer, M.D., et al. "Effect of Unsaturated Fats upon Lipemia and Conjunctival Circulation." *Journal of the American Medical Association* 193 (1965): 110.

Horton, Edward S., M.D. "Effects of Low Energy Diets on Work Performance." *American Journal of Clinical Nutrition* 35 (May 1982): 1228–33.

Knisely, Melvin H., et al. "Sludged Blood." *Science* (November 7, 1947): 431.

Regan, Timothy J., M.D., et al. "Myocardial Blood Flow and Oxygen Consumption During Postprandial Lipemia and Heparin-induced Lipolysis." *Circulation* 23 (January 1961).

Swank, Roy L. "Changes in Blood Produced by a Fat Meal and by Intravenous Heparin." *American Journal of Physiology* 164 (1951): 798.

———. "Oxygen Availability in Brain Tissue After Lipid Meals." *American Journal of Physiology* 198 (1960): 217.

Williams, Arthur V., M.D., et al. "Increased Blood Cell Agglutination Following Ingestion of Fat." *Anthology* 8 (1957): 29.

DMG

Archer, Michael C. Critique of paper by Colman et al, "Mutagenicity of N,N-Dimethylglycine When Mixed with Nitrite: Possible Significance in Human Use of Pangamates." Critique available from FoodScience Laboratories, 20 New England Drive, Essex Junction, VT 05452.

Charles, Anne. "DMG Proving To Be Valuable Aid in Competition." *Horse World* (October 1982): 20.

Colman, Neville, and Herbert, Victor, et al. "Mutagenicity of N,N-Dimethylglycine When Mixed with Nitrite: Possible Significance in Human Use of Pangamates." *Proceedings of the Society for Experimental Biology and Medicine* 164 (May 1980).

Freed, William J. "Prevention of Strychnine-Induced Seizures and Death by the N-Methylated Glycine Derivatives Betaine, N,N-Dimethylglycine and Sarcosine." *Pharmacology, Biochemistry and Behavior* 22 (1985): 641–43.

Gannon, James. R., B.V.Sc. (Sundown Greyhound Racing Club Veterinary Clinic). "A Clinical Evaluation of N,N-Dimethylglycine (DMG) and Diisopropylammonium Dichloroacetate (DIPA) on the Performance of Racing Greyhounds." *Canine Practice* 9 (No. 6, Nov.–Dec. 1982).

Graber, Charles D. et al. "Immunomodulating Properties of N,N-Dimethylglycine in Humans." *Journal of Infectious Diseases* 143 (No. 1, January 1981): 101.

Kleinkopf, Karl (track coach, College of Southern Idaho). "N,N-Dimethylglycine Hydrochloride and Calcium Gluconate and Its Effect on Maximum Oxygen Consumption on Highly Conditioned Athletes." Report dated July 1980, available from FoodScience Laboratories, 20 New England Drive, Essex Junction, VT 05452.

Levine, Steve B., D.V.M., et al. "Effect of a Nutritional Supplement Containing N,N-Dimethylglycine (DMG) on the Racing Standardbred." *Equine Practice* 4 (No. 3, March 1982).

Meduski, Jerzy, M.D., Ph.D., "Effect of Dietary N,N-Dimethylglycine on the Uptake of Molecular Oxygen in Sprague-Dawley Rats." Study available from FoodScience Laboratories, 20 New England Drive, Essex Junction, VT 05452.

———. "Retardation of Lactic Acid by N,N-Dimethylglycine (DMG)." Paper presented at Pacific Slope Conference, University of California, San Diego, July 7–9, 1980.

———. "Nutritional Evaluation of the Results of the 157-Day Subchronical Estimation of N,N-Dimethylglycine Toxicity." Report dated December 11, 1979, available from FoodScience Laboratories, 20 New England Drive, Essex Junction, VT 05452.

Reap, E. A., and Lawson, J. W. "The Effects of Dimethylglycine on the Immune Response of Rabbits." Official Abstract, 1987 ASM Annual Meeting, Atlanta, Georgia, March 1–6, 1987.

Roach, Steve, M.D. "N,N-Dimethylglycine for Epilepsy" (letter). *Journal of the American Medical Association* (October 21, 1982).

Ward, Thomas N., M.D., et al. "Dimethylglycine and Reduction of Mortality in Penicillin-Induced Seizures." *Annals of Neurology* 17 (No. 2, February 1985): 213.

Ginseng and Siberian Ginseng

Forgo, I., M.D. "Doping Control of Top-Ranking Athletes After a 14-Day Treatment with Ginsana." Interner Bericht vom 13.2.80. Study available from Ginsana USA, 50 Maple Place, Manhasset, NY 11030.

———. "Effect of a Standardized Ginseng Extract on General Well-Being, Reaction Capacity, Pulmonary Function and Gonadal Hormones." *Medizinische Welt* 32 (No. 19, 1981): 751–756.

———. "On the Question of Influencing the Performance of Top Sportsmen by Means of Biologically Active Substances." *Aerztliche Praxis* 33 (No. 44, 1981): 1784–86.

Halstead, Bruce W., M.D. "*Eleutherococcus Senticosus. Siberian Ginseng: An Introduction to the Concept of Adaptogenic Medicine.* Book available from Oriental Healing Arts Institute, 1945 Palo Verde Avenue, Suite 208, Long Beach, California.

Hess, E. G. et al. "Effects of Subchronic Feeding of Ginseng Extract G115 in Beagle Dogs." *Food and Chemical Toxicology* 21 (No. 1, 1983): 95–97.

———. "Reproduction Study in Rats of Ginseng Extract G115." *Food and Chemical Toxicology* 20 (No. 2, 1982): 189–92.

Ng, T. B., and Yeung, H. W. "Hypoglycemic Constituents of Panax Ginseng." *General Pharmacology* 16 (No. 6, 1985): 549–52.

Quiroga, Hector A., M.D., et al. "The Effect of Panax Ginseng Extract on Cerebrovascular Deficits." *Orientation Medica* 28 1208 (1979): 86–87. Study available from Ginsana USA, 50 Maple Place, Manhasset, NY 11030.

Savel, J. "Pharmacological Investigation of the Standardized Ginseng Extract G115." Available from Ginsana USA, 50 Maple Place, Manhasset, NY 11030.

Schmidt, U. J., et al. "Pharmacotherapy and So-called Basic Therapy in Old Age." Paper presented at the International Congress of Gerontology, Tokyo, Japan, August 20–25, 1978.

L-carnitine

Bell, Frank, et al. "An Inverse Relationship Between Plasma Carnitine and Triglycerides in Selected *Macaca arctoides* and *Macaca nemistrina* Fed a Low-Fat Chow Diet." *Comparative Biochemical Physiology* 78B (No. 2, 1984): 311–14.

Kendler, Barry, S., Ph.D. "Carnitine: An Overview of Its Role in Preventive Medicine." *Preventive Medicine* 15 (1986): 373–90.

Lennon, Doris, et al. "Interorgan Cooperativity in Carnitine Metabolism." *American Physiological Society* (1986).

Maebashi, M., et al. "Lipid-Lowering Effect of Carnitine in Patients with Type-IV Hyperlipoproteinaemia." *Lancet* (October 14, 1978): 805.

Marconi, C., et al. "Effects of L-carnitine Loading on the Aerobic and Anaerobic Performance of Endurance Athletes." *European Journal of Applied Physiology* 54 (1985): 131–35.

Mitchell, Madeleine, Ph.D. "Carnitine Metabolism in Human Subjects." *American Journal of Clinical Nutrition* 31 (April 1978): 645–59.

Vacha, Gian Maria, M.D., et al. "Favorable Effects of L-carnitine Treatment on Hypertriglyceridemia in Hemodialysis Patients." *American Journal of Clinical Nutrition* 38 (October 1983): 352.

Index

COOKING? DIETING? HERE'S HELP!

THE FOOD ALLERGY COOKBOOK
Allergy Information Association
_____ 90185-2 $4.95 U.S.

EASY, SWEET AND SUGARFREE
Karen E. Barkie
_____ 90282-4 $3.50 U.S.   _____ 90283-2 $4.50 Can.

BLOOMINGDALE'S EAT HEALTHY DIET
Laura Stein
_____ 90641-2 $3.95 U.S.   _____ 90642-0 $4.95 Can.

MARY ELLEN'S HELP YOURSELF DIET PLAN
Mary Ellen Pinkham
_____ 90237-9 $2.95 U.S.   _____ 90238-7 $3.95 Can.

THE BOOK OF WHOLE GRAINS
Marlene Anne Bumgarner
_____ 90072-4 $4.95 U.S.   _____ 90073-2 $6.25 Can.

Publishers Book and Audio Mailing Service
P.O. Box 120159, Staten Island, NY 10312-0004

Please send me the book(s) I have checked above. I am enclosing
$ _____ (please add $1.25 for the first book, and $.25 for each
additional book to cover postage and handling. Send check or
money order only—no CODs.)

Name _____

Address _____

City _____ State/Zip _____

Please allow six weeks for delivery. Prices subject to change
without notice.

CD 1/89

Self-Help Guides

from St. Martin's Paperbacks

HOW TO SAVE YOUR TROUBLED MARRIAGE
Cristy Lane and Dr. Laura Ann Stevens
_____ 91360-5 $3.50 U.S. _____ 91361-3 $4.50 Can.

THE WAY UP FROM DOWN
Priscilla Slagle, M.D.
_____ 91106-8 $4.50 U.S. _____ 91107-6 $5.50 Can.

IN SEARCH OF MYSELF AND OTHER CHILDREN
Eda Le Shan
_____ 91272-2 $3.50 U.S. _____ 91273-0 $4.50 Can.

LOOK BEFORE YOU LOVE
Melissa Sands
_____ 90672-2 $3.95 U.S. _____ 90673-0 $4.95 Can.

SELF-ESTEEM
Mathew McKay and Patrick Fanning
_____ 90443-6 $4.95 U.S. _____ 90444-4 $5.95 Can.

Publishers Book and Audio Mailing Service
P.O. Box 120159, Staten Island, NY 10312-0004

Please send me the book(s) I have checked above. I am enclosing
$ _____ (please add $1.25 for the first book, and $.25 for each
additional book to cover postage and handling. Send check or
money order only—no CODs.)

Name _____

Address _____

City _____ State/Zip _____

Please allow six weeks for delivery. Prices subject to change
without notice.

LANDMARK BESTSELLERS
FROM ST. MARTIN'S PAPERBACKS